Collins

AQA GCSE (9–1) Biology topics for Combined Science

Foundation Support Workbook

Liz Ouldridge

William Collins' dream of knowledge for all began with the publication of his first book in 1819. A self-educated mill worker, he not only enriched millions of lives, but also founded a flourishing publishing house. Today, staying true to this spirit, Collins books are packed with inspiration, innovation and practical expertise. They place you at the centre of a world of possibility and give you exactly what you need to explore it.

Collins. Freedom to teach

HarperCollins Publishers
The News Building
1 London Bridge Street
London SE1 9GF

**Browse the complete Collins catalogue at
www.collins.co.uk**

First edition 2016

10 9 8 7 6 5 4 3 2

© HarperCollins Publishers 2016

ISBN 978-0-00-818954-9

Collins® is a registered trademark of HarperCollins Publishers Limited

www.collins.co.uk

A catalogue record for this book is available from the British Library

Commissioned by Gillian Lindsey
Project managed by Sarah Thomas
Copy edited by Rebecca Ramsden
Proofread by Amanda Harman
Technical review by Rich Cutler
Typeset by Jouve India Pvt Ltd.,
Cover design by We are Laura and Jouve
Cover image: 123rf/Alexey Ukhov
Printed and bound by Printing Express, Hong Kong

The publisher would also like to thank Linda Needham and Richard Needham for their support in the development of this book.

Introduction

This workbook will help you build your confidence in answering Biology questions for GCSE Combined Science, Foundation tier.

It gives you practice in using key scientific words, writing longer answers and applying maths and practical skills.

The opening summary shows what definitions you need to learn.

Learn how to answer test questions by seeing part of the answer filled in.

This will help you develop the skills you need to write longer answers, or to use maths in science.

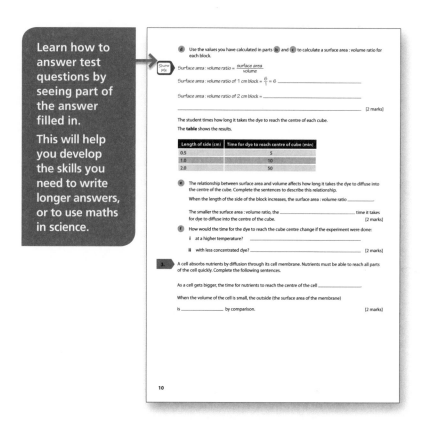

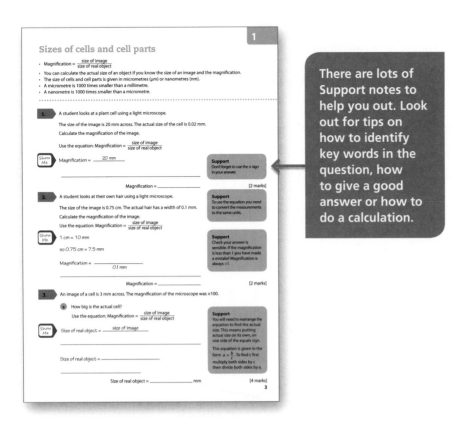

There are lots of Support notes to help you out. Look out for tips on how to identify key words in the question, how to give a good answer or how to do a calculation.

The amount of support gradually decreases throughout the workbook. As you build your skills you should be able to complete more of the questions yourself.

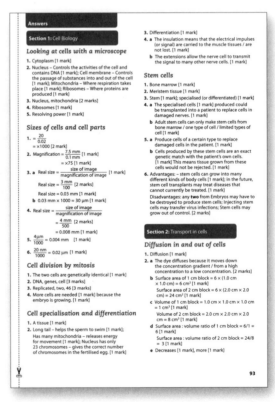

There are answers to all the questions at the back of the book. You can check your answers yourself or your teacher might tear them out and give them to you later to mark your work.

Contents

Looking at cells with a microscope

- Cells can be studied using light microscopes and electron microscopes.
- An electron microscope can magnify more than a light microscope.
  (They can make cells look much bigger.)
- An electron microscope also has a higher resolving power. (They show more detail.)
- Cells contain small structures that do different jobs.
- Bacterial cells are much smaller and simpler than plant and animal cells.

1. Where in the cell do most chemical reactions take place? Tick **one** box.

☐ Cell membrane   ☑ Cytoplasm   ☐ Nucleus   [1 mark]

2. Draw **one** line from each cell structure to the correct job.

Cell structure   **Job**

| Nucleus |
| Cell membrane |
| Mitochondria |
| Ribosomes |

| Where respiration takes place |
| Controls the activities of the cell and contains DNA |
| Where proteins are produced |
| Controls the transport of substances into and out of the cell |

[4 marks]

3. Name **two** cell structures from the list in question 2 that are **not** found in bacterial cells.

1 _Ribosomes_   2 _mitochondria_   [2 marks]

4. Complete the sentence. Use a word from the box.

| Nucleus   Ribosomes |

Some parts of a cell such as _Ribosomes_ can only be seen with an electron microscope.   [1 mark]

5. Complete the sentence. Use a word from the box.

| Resolving power   Magnification |

The electron microscope shows more detail than a light microscope. This is because the electron

microscope has a higher _magnification_.   [1 mark]

Sizes of cells and cell parts

- Magnification = $\dfrac{\text{size of image}}{\text{size of real object}}$

- You can calculate the actual size of an object if you know the size of an image and the magnification.
- The size of cells and cell parts is given in micrometres (μm) or nanometres (nm).
- A micrometre is 1000 times smaller than a millimetre.
- A nanometre is 1000 times smaller than a micrometre.

---

1. A student looks at a plant cell using a light microscope.

The size of the image is 20 mm across. The actual size of the cell is 0.02 mm.

Calculate the magnification of the image.

Use the equation: Magnification = $\dfrac{\text{size of image}}{\text{size of real object}}$

 Magnification = _____20 mm_____

Support
Don't forget to use the × sign in your answer.

_____

Magnification = _____ [2 marks]

2. A student looks at their own hair using a light microscope.

Support
To use the equation you need to convert the measurements to the same units.

The size of the image is 0.75 cm. The actual hair has a width of 0.1 mm.

Calculate the magnification of the image.

Use the equation: Magnification = $\dfrac{\text{size of image}}{\text{size of real object}}$

 1 cm = 10 mm

so 0.75 cm = 7.5 mm

Support
Check your answer is sensible. If the magnification is less than 1 you have made a mistake! Magnification is always >1.

Magnification = $\dfrac{}{0.1\ mm}$

_____

Magnification = _____ [2 marks]

3. An image of a cell is 3 mm across. The magnification of the microscope was ×100.

a How big is the actual cell?

Use the equation: Magnification = $\dfrac{\text{size of image}}{\text{size of real object}}$

 Size of real object = $\dfrac{\text{size of image}}{}$

_____

Size of real object = _____

_____

Support
You will need to rearrange the equation to find the actual size. This means putting actual size on its own, on one side of the equals sign.

This equation is given in the form $a = \dfrac{b}{c}$. To find c first multiply both sides by c then divide both sides by a.

Size of real object = _____ mm [4 marks]

b How big is the cell in micrometres (µm)?

Show Me 1 mm = 1000 µm

Real size of cell = _____ × 1000

_____

Real size of cell = _____ µm   [1 mark]

4. A scientist looks at red blood cells with a microscope. In the image, the size of one red blood cell is 4 mm.

The magnification is ×500.

How big is the real cell?

_____

_____

_____

Real size = _____ mm   [3 marks]

5. A bacterium is 4 µm in length.

Change the length into millimetres (mm). Give your answer in decimal form.

Show Me $1 \, \mu m = \frac{1}{1000} \, mm$

_____

so $4 \, \mu m = \frac{4}{1000} \, mm$

_____

Length = _____ mm   [1 mark]

6. A ribosome is 20 nm across.

Change the length into micrometres (µm). Give your answer in decimal form.

_____

Length = _____ µm   [1 mark]

Support
Nanometres are **smaller** than millimetres. To convert from a smaller unit to a larger unit, divide. So to convert from 20 nm to µm you divide 20 by 1000.

Cell division by mitosis

- New cells are needed as an organism grows or to repair damaged tissues.
- A cell grows in size, the DNA replicates, then the cell divides into two. Each cell grows in size, and the cycle repeats. This is called the cell cycle.
- The process of how cells divide in two is called mitosis.
- The nucleus of a cell contains chromosomes.
- Chromosomes are made from DNA and carry the genes.

1. When a cell divides by mitosis, two new cells are formed. What can you say about the genes in the new cells?

Tick **one** box.

☐ The two cells are genetically different   ☑ The two cells are genetically identical   [1 mark]

2. The nucleus of every cell contains chromosomes.

Complete the following sentences.

Chromosomes are made from a substance called _____. Each chromosome

contains many sets of instructions called _____. These control the activities

of the _____.   [3 marks]

3. Human body cells have 46 chromosomes.

Complete the following sentences.

Show Me   Before a cell can divide the chromosomes must be <u>replicated</u>.

There are now _____ copies of each chromosome.

After cell division there are _____ chromosomes in each cell.   [3 marks]

4. Explain why mitosis must occur in a developing human embryo.

_____

_____   [2 marks]

> **Support**
> You need to **explain why**, which means you have to link what happens to the reason. Use words that link one part of each sentence to the next part, such as 'because'.

Cell specialisation and differentiation

- As an organism develops the cells become specialised into different types.
- This is called differentiation.
- Sperm cells, nerve cells and muscle cells are all examples of specialised cells in animals.
- They have special structures that help them do their job.
- Groups of the same type of cell are called tissues.

1. What is the name for a group of similar cells?

Tick **one** box.

☐ An organ ☐ A system ☐ A tissue [1 mark]

2. A sperm cell is a specialised sex cell.

Draw **one** line from each feature of a sperm cell to the correct explanation of how this helps the sperm cell do its job.

Feature	Explanation
Long tail	Releases energy for movement
Has many mitochondria	Gives the correct number of chromosomes in the fertilised egg
Nucleus has only 23 chromosomes	Helps the sperm to swim

[3 marks]

3. What is the name of the process by which unspecialised cells become specialised for a particular function?

_____ [1 mark]

4. The diagram shows a motor nerve cell. This type of cell carries electrical signals to muscle cells. The motor nerve cell has special structures to help it do its job.

Explain how each of the structures listed below help the nerve cell do its job.

a A nerve cell is surrounded by a fatty substance which is an insulator.

Show Me

The insulation means that

_____

_____ [1 mark]

nerve cell
1 m

b There are many small extensions coming from the main part of the cell.

_____ [1 mark]

Stem cells

- Stem cells are unspecialised cells. They can become many different types of cells, which are then specialised.
- Animal embryos that are a few days old are made up of stem cells.
- Stem cells are also found in some parts of adult animals, such as bone marrow, where they make new blood cells.
- In the future, stem cells may be used to grow replacement cells to treat, for example, diabetes and paralysis.
- Plants also have these cells that can become other types of cells. They are found in particular tissues called meristems.
- A clone is genetically identical to the organism it is cloned from.

1. Where are stem cells found in the body?

Tick **one** box.

☐ Blood   ☐ Bone marrow   ☐ Heart   [1 mark]

2. Name the type of tissue where stem cells are found in plants.

_____ [1 mark]

> **Support**
> **Stem** has two meanings in biology. **Plant stems** are an example of plant organs. **Stem cells** are the source of new **cells** to build tissues and **organs.**

3. As a human embryo develops, different types of cells such as muscle or blood cells are produced.

Complete the sentences.

All the cells in an early embryo are _____ cells. These cells can become any type of

_____ cell. [2 marks]

4. Stem cells can be extracted from embryos. Large numbers of these stem cells can be grown in the laboratory and made to produce specialised cells like nerve cells.

   a Explain how stem cells could be used to treat patients with damaged nerves.

> Show Me

The _____ produced could be transplanted into a

patient's _____ [2 marks]

   b Explain why stem cells from bone marrow cannot be used to treat patients with damaged nerves.

> Show Me

Adult stem cells from bone marrow can only make

_____ [1 mark]

5. Stem cells have been produced using a process called therapeutic cloning. These stem cells have the same genetic material as a cell in the patient's body.

a What do scientists do with these stem cells?

Tick **one** box.

☐ Produce a clone of a person

☐ Produce embryos for fertility treatment

☐ Produce cells of a certain type to replace damaged cells in the patient [1 mark]

b Explain the benefit to the patient of using stem cells produced this way.

Show Me

Cells produced by these stem cells _____

_____

This means tissue grown from these cells _____ [2 marks]

6. Some statements about using human stem cells are given below.

Tick **two** advantages and **two** disadvantages of using stem cells to treat humans.

Statement	Advantage	Disadvantage
Embryos may have to be destroyed to produce stem cells.		
In the future, stem cell transplants may treat diseases that cannot currently be treated.		
Stem cells can grow into many different kinds of body cells.		
Injecting stem cells may transfer virus infections.		
Stem cells may grow out of control.		

[4 marks]

Diffusion in and out of cells

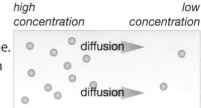

high concentration | low concentration

- Substances can move in and out of cells by diffusion through the cell membrane.
- In diffusion, substances move from a high concentration to a low concentration until all areas have an equal concentration.
- The rate of diffusion increases if the difference in concentration is bigger, or if the temperature increases.
- Size affects how quickly nutrients can diffuse into a cell.
- Smaller cells have a larger surface area to volume ratio. This is better for getting nutrients into the cell.

1. How do gases move into or out of a leaf?

Tick **one** box.

☐ Active transport   ☐ Diffusion   ☐ Osmosis   [1 mark]

2. A student carries out an experiment with agar cubes of different sizes. They place the cubes in a coloured dye. The dye moves into the cubes.

a Explain why the dye moves into the cubes.

Show Me

The dye _____

because _____ [2 marks]

> **Support**
> This question asks you to **explain why**. This often means you should use the word 'because' in your answer. It is also important to use science key words. Try to use the words 'diffusion' and 'concentrated'.

As the size of the cubes increases, so does their volume and surface area.

b Use the equation below to calculate the surface area of the different sized cubes.

Show Me

Surface area of cube = 6 × area of one face

Surface area of 1 cm block = 6 × (1.0 cm × 1.0 cm)

= 6 cm²

Surface area of 2 cm block = _____

> **Support**
> To find surface area, start by finding the area of one face (a square). Then count the number of faces on a cube. Then find the surface area of the whole cube.

_____

_____ cm²   [2 marks]

c Use the equation below to calculate the volume of the different sized cubes.

Volume of a cube = length × width × height

Show Me

Volume of 1 cm block = (1.0 cm × 1.0 cm × 1.0 cm)

= 1 cm³

Volume of 2 cm block = _____

_____

= _____ cm³   [2 marks]

d Use the values you have calculated in parts **b** and **c** to calculate a surface area : volume ratio for each block.

Show Me ▶ Surface area : volume ratio = $\dfrac{\text{surface area}}{\text{volume}}$

Surface area : volume ratio of 1 cm block = $\dfrac{6}{1}$ = 6 _____

Surface area : volume ratio of 2 cm block = _____

_____ [2 marks]

The student times how long it takes the dye to reach the centre of each cube.

The **table** shows the results.

Length of side (cm)	Time for dye to reach centre of cube (min)
0.5	5
1.0	10
2.0	50

e The relationship between surface area and volume affects how long it takes the dye to diffuse into the centre of the cube. Complete the sentences to describe this relationship.

When the length of the side of the block increases, the surface area : volume ratio _____.

The smaller the surface area : volume ratio, the _____ time it takes for dye to diffuse into the centre of the cube. [2 marks]

f How would the time for the dye to reach the cube centre change if the experiment were done:

i at a higher temperature? _____

ii with less concentrated dye? _____ [2 marks]

3. ▶ A cell absorbs nutrients by diffusion through its cell membrane. Nutrients must be able to reach all parts of the cell quickly. Complete the following sentences.

As a cell gets bigger, the time for nutrients to reach the centre of the cell _____.

When the volume of the cell is small, the outside (the surface area of the membrane)

is _____ by comparison. [2 marks]

Exchange surfaces in animals

- Substances move into or out of the blood at specialised exchange surfaces.
- Examples of exchange surfaces include air sacs (alveoli) in the lungs, villi in the small intestine, and the gills of fish.
- The surfaces are adapted so substances can be exchanged quickly by diffusion.
- The rate of diffusion is increased by having a large surface area or being very thin so the diffusion distance is very short.
- The rate of diffusion is also increased if the substance is removed quickly by a good blood supply.

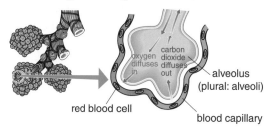

gas exchange in an air sac

oxygen diffuses in

carbon dioxide diffuses out

red blood cell

alveolus (plural: alveoli)

blood capillary

1. Mammal lungs exchange gases with the animal's environment.

a Which gas is taken in by the lungs?

_____ [1 mark]

b Explain why this gas moves from the air sacs of the lungs into the blood.

Show Me

The concentration of _____

_____

_____

Support
There are **4 marks** so you need to make four points. Diffusion is a key word for this topic but you need to say what diffuses, and where it diffuses **from** and **to**.

so _____ diffuses from _____

_____ to _____. [4 marks]

2. Give **two** ways alveoli in the lungs are adapted for their function.

1 _____

2 _____ [2 marks]

3. Human lungs are made up of about 500 million small air sacs called alveoli. They give a large surface area for gas exchange.

Why is it important for the lungs to have such a large surface area?

_____

_____

_____

_____ [2 marks]

4. The gills in fish exchange gases with water.

The diagram shows that the gills of a fish are near its mouth. It also shows the structure of a gill.

a Explain how the feathery structure of gills helps with their function of exchanging gases.

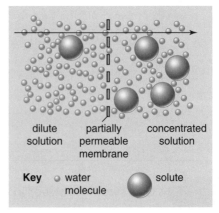

_____

_____

[1 mark]

b Organs where gases are exchanged, such as gills, need a good blood supply. This makes the gills look red.

Complete the sentences about gills.

The blood in the gills takes _____ into the body and brings _____ back

to be removed. These substances pass into the water by _____. [3 marks]

Osmosis

- Cell membranes are partially permeable – they have tiny holes that only let small molecules pass through.
- Osmosis is a special case of diffusion where water diffuses from a dilute solution to a concentrated solution through a partially permeable membrane.
- Water moves across cell membranes by osmosis.

1. Some students are using plastic tubing in an experiment to show how substances move into and out of cells. The tubing is made into a bag so that it is like the cell membrane.

The tubing has small holes. The holes allow water molecules to pass through but sugar molecules are too big to pass through.

This is the method used.

① Set up two bags of tubing containing the same volume of solution. One bag should contain a dilute solution of sugar and the other bag a concentrated solution of sugar.

② Weigh each bag and record the mass.

③ Place both bags in distilled water.

④ Every 10 minutes take the bags out and dry the outsides.
Weigh each bag and record the mass.

The graph shows their results.

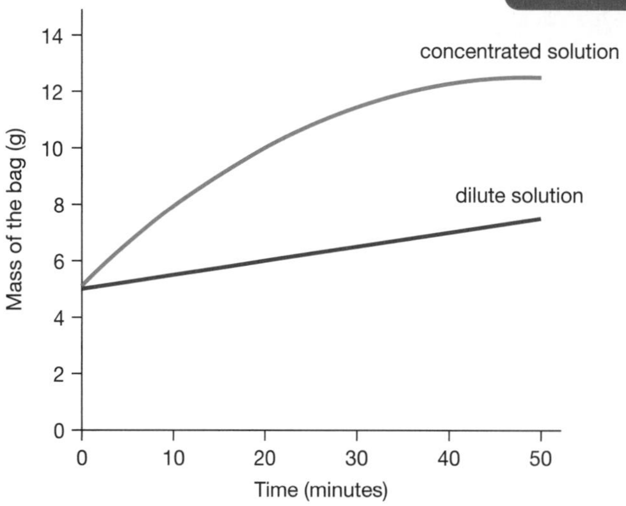

a Describe the results of the experiment.

_____

_____

[2 marks]

b What causes the change in mass of the tubing?

Show Me

Water molecules move _____

Because _____

_____

_____

_____

[3 marks]

Support
Look at what is happening to the mass of the bag in a dilute solution, does it increase or decrease? Now look at the mass of the bag in a concentrated solution. Does it have the same pattern?

c The bag in the dilute solution started with a mass of 5 g and finished with a mass of 7.5 g. What is the percentage change in mass?

Show Me

$$\text{Percentage change in mass} = \frac{\text{change in mass}}{\text{starting mass}} \times 100$$

Change in mass = 7.5 g – 5 g or 2.5 g

$$\text{Percentage change in mass} = \frac{2.5}{5} \times 100$$

Support
In questions like this you need to apply what you know to a problem you have not seen before. Look for clues in the information about the experiment. What was in the mixture put into each bag, and what could be diffusing?

Percentage change in mass = _____% [3 marks]

d The bag in the concentrated solution started with a mass of 5.1 g and finished with a mass of 12.5 g.

What is the percentage change in mass?

_____

_____

_____

Percentage change in mass = _____ % [3 marks]

Active transport

- Some substances that living cells need can be moved against a concentration gradient – from a concentrated solution to a more dilute solution.
- Active transport needs energy from respiration.
- Plant roots absorb minerals from the soil water by active transport.
- Sugar molecules are absorbed from the gut into the blood by active transport.

1. Which process uses energy? Tick **one** box.

☐ Diffusion ☐ Active transport [1 mark]

2. Diffusion and active transport are two ways that materials can be transported across cell membranes.

Complete the sentences below. Use words from the box. Each word can be used once, more than once or not at all.

Diffusion Active transport

_____ moves substances down their concentration gradient (from a high concentration to a lower concentration).

_____ moves substances against their concentration gradient (from a low concentration to a higher concentration).

When the concentration of sugar molecules in the gut is lower than in the blood, sugar moves into the

blood by _____. [3 marks]

3. Osmosis is another method of transport across cell membranes.

Compare osmosis and active transport.

Show Me

Active transport needs energy to transport substances but osmosis does not.

_____

_____

_____

> **Support**
> A **compare** question means give similarities **and** differences. You will need to mention both parts in the comparison. Good words to use in your answers are 'both', 'however', 'whereas' and 'but'. Remember, **3 marks** means three comparisons are needed.

[3 marks]

4. Plant roots absorb mineral ions from the soil. Usually, the concentration of minerals in the soil solution outside the roots is very low.

Explain how roots can absorb mineral ions **against** the concentration gradient.

_____

_____ [2 marks]

The digestive system

- Specialised cells are organised into tissues, tissues into organs and organs into organ systems.
- The digestive system is the organ system that digests and absorbs food.
- The salivary glands, stomach, pancreas and small intestine produce enzymes to break down food.
- The liver produces bile. Bile released in the small intestine separates fat (lipids) into small droplets to make it easier to digest.
- Bile is alkaline. This helps those digestive enzymes that cannot work in acid conditions.

1. Which organ produces bile to neutralise stomach acid and emulsify fat?

_____ [1 mark]

2. The box below shows the levels of organisation in the body. Use words from the box to give examples for each level.

Stomach	Muscle tissue	Digestive system	Muscle cells

The first one has been done for you.

Cell   ➡   Tissue   ➡   Organ   ➡   Organ system

__Muscle cells__   _____   _____   _____ [3 marks]

3. **a** Which enzyme is produced by salivary glands?

_____ [1 mark]

b Give **two** other organs that produce enzymes.

i _____ **ii** _____ [2 marks]

4. Each organ in the digestive system has a specific function.

Complete the sentences. Use words from the box.

Large intestine	Stomach	Small intestine	Pancreas	Gall bladder

The _____ stores the bile before releasing it into the small intestine.

The _____ mixes food, produces hydrochloric acid to kill microbes and produces proteases to break down proteins in our food.

The _____ produces carbohydrases, lipases and proteases for release into the small intestine.

The _____ also produces carbohydrases, lipases and proteases to complete digestion.

[4 marks]

Digestive enzymes

- Enzymes are biological catalysts. They speed up chemical reactions.
- Digestive enzymes break down big molecules into small molecules that can be absorbed into the blood.
- The body uses these small molecules for respiration and to build new substances needed for growth.
- All enzymes have an active site. This is a part of the enzyme that will fit into a particular molecule, just as a key will only fit into one lock. This is the 'lock and key theory'.
- The 'lock and key theory' means each enzyme will only catalyse one reaction.
- Temperature and pH affect how quickly enzymes work.

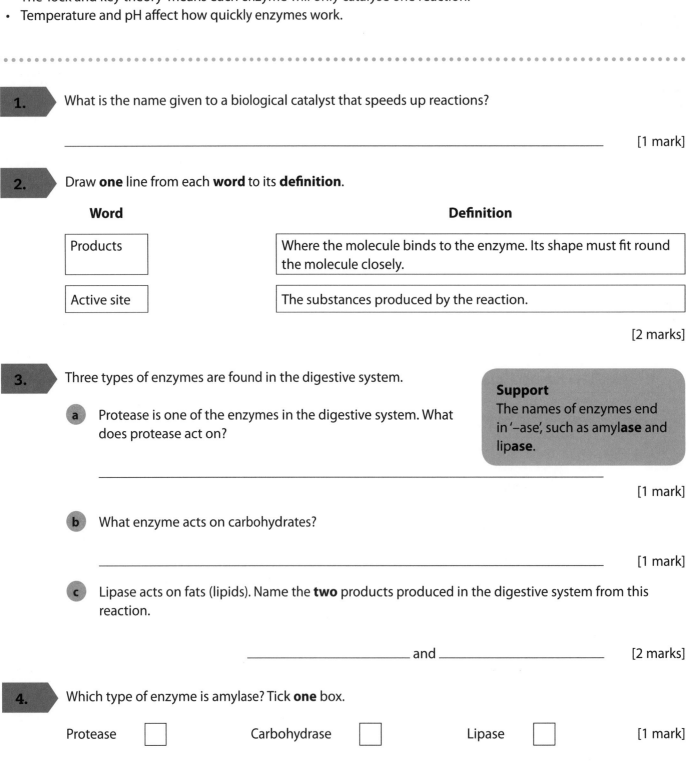

1. What is the name given to a biological catalyst that speeds up reactions?

_____ [1 mark]

2. Draw **one** line from each **word** to its **definition**.

Word	Definition
Products	Where the molecule binds to the enzyme. Its shape must fit round the molecule closely.
Active site	The substances produced by the reaction.

[2 marks]

3. Three types of enzymes are found in the digestive system.

> **Support**
> The names of enzymes end in '–ase', such as amyl**ase** and lip**ase**.

a Protease is one of the enzymes in the digestive system. What does protease act on?

_____ [1 mark]

b What enzyme acts on carbohydrates?

_____ [1 mark]

c Lipase acts on fats (lipids). Name the **two** products produced in the digestive system from this reaction.

_____ and _____ [2 marks]

4. Which type of enzyme is amylase? Tick **one** box.

Protease ☐   Carbohydrase ☐   Lipase ☐   [1 mark]

5. A student carried out an experiment to see how long it took to digest starch at different temperatures. They used the enzyme amylase.

a Name the dependent variable and suggest **one** control variable in this investigation.

_____

_____ [2 marks]

The student's results are shown in the table.

The rate of reaction can be calculated using this equation:

$$\text{Rate of reaction} = \frac{\text{mass of starch digested}}{\text{digestion time}}$$

b Calculate the rate of reaction for each temperature. One has been done for you.

Temperature (°C)	Mass of starch (g)	Digestion time (mins)	Rate of reaction (g/min)
20	5	10	Rate = 5/10 = 0.5
30	5	7	
40	5	5	
50	5	40	

_____ [4 marks]

c Describe the trend in digestion rate shown in the completed table.

_____

_____

Support
A **trend** in results means a pattern. There are **2 marks** so don't just say 'it goes up' or 'it goes down'. Use numbers from the table in your answer.

[2 marks]

d Suggest why it takes much longer to digest the starch at 50 °C than at 40 °C.

_____

_____

_____

Support
Enzymes work best at body temperature. They change shape at high temperatures.

[2 marks]

Factors affecting enzymes

- The rate of enzyme reactions is affected by temperature and pH.
- Amylase breaks down starch to form sugars.
- Starch can be detected by using iodine.
- This means a starch test can be used to see if starch has been completely digested. When the starch is digested the iodine will no longer turn blue-black, it will stay yellow.

1. A student is planning an experiment to find out how pH affects the activity of the enzyme amylase. The student completed the table below to help them plan.

Key variable	What I have chosen?	How I will do this?
Independent variable (Change this in the experiment)	The pH of the enzyme reaction mixture	Add some **buffer solution** to the reaction mixture. This will keep the pH at a certain value. Use a **range** of buffer solutions from pH 3 to pH 8. Check the results are **repeatable** by doing each pH value three times.
Dependent variable (Measure this this to find the result)	The time taken for the starch to be broken down	After mixing the amylase and the starch together, take a sample every 15 seconds and add a drop to some **iodine solution** placed in the well of a spotting tile. The iodine will go blue-black if starch is present. **Record the time** taken for the iodine to stop changing colour.
Control variables (Keep these the same to make a fair test)	• Temperature • Volume and concentration of enzyme • Volume and concentration of reaction mixture	• Use an **electric water bath** set to 37 °C to keep the temperature constant. Warm the amylase and starch before mixing. • Use the same batch of enzyme, add 2 cm³ of this solution each time. • Use 1% starch solution, add 5 cm³ each time.

Using the information in the table, describe a method you could use to investigate how pH affects the activity of amylase.

You should include what variables you will control and what you will measure.

Support
Thinking about the key variables involved is often a good way to plan an experiment.

Support
Read through the table and think about the order of things you would do in the experiment.
You need to prepare the equipment first and then perform the experiment.

Show Me

First, prepare the spotting tile by adding a drop of iodine to each well.

Set the _____ *to 37 °C and place* _____

_____

_____

_____

_____

_____

_____

_____

_____

_____ [6 marks]

The heart and blood vessels

- The heart pumps blood around the body.
- Blood leaves the heart in arteries and returns to the heart in veins.
- The aorta is the main artery. The vena cava is the main vein.
- A network of capillaries connects the arteries and the veins.
- Each type of blood vessel is adapted to its function.
- A group of cells in the heart controls beating of the whole heart and so acts as a natural pacemaker.

Arteries — thick, elastic wall, small central hole

Veins — thin wall, large central hole, valve

Capillaries — single-cell wall

1. Complete the sentences below.

The circulatory system is made up of the _____, arteries, veins and capillaries.

The heart pumps blood around the body. It is made of a strong _____ which contracts and relaxes continuously. [2 marks]

2. Arteries carry high pressure blood away from the heart.

a Which blood vessel carries low pressure blood back to the heart?

_____ [1 mark]

b Which blood vessel connects arteries and veins?

_____ [1 mark]

3. Complete the sentences below.

Use words from the box.

Aorta   Vena cava

The main artery leaving the heart is the _____.

The main vein in which blood returns to the heart is the _____. [2 marks]

4. Arteries, veins and capillaries have different structures because they are adapted to carry out slightly different functions.

a Explain **one** feature of arteries that is related to their function.

Show Me

Arteries have _____ so they can

_____ when blood is pumped under high pressure. [2 marks]

b Explain **one** feature of capillaries that is related to their function.

Show Me

Capillaries have _____ so they can exchange

_____. [2 marks]

c Veins have valves. Explain how this feature is related to their function.

_____

_____ [1 mark]

Heart–lungs system

- The heart is part of a double circulatory system. It contains two separate pumps.
- The right ventricle pumps blood from the body to the lungs.
- The left ventricle pumps blood from the lungs to the rest of the body.
- In the lungs oxygen diffuses into the blood. Carbon dioxide diffuses out of the blood.
- The lungs have a large surface area for gas exchange.
- Red blood cells transport oxygen. They have features to help them do this.

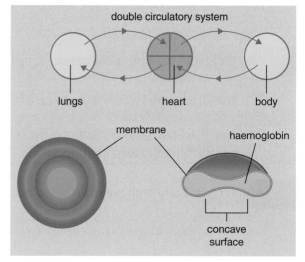

double circulatory system

lungs   heart   body

membrane   haemoglobin

concave surface

1. Complete the sentences below.

The pulmonary artery goes from the heart to the _____.

The pulmonary vein goes back into the _____ from the lungs. [2 marks]

2. The diagram below shows how blood flows through the heart.

The following sentences describe how the blood flows through the heart. The sentences are in the wrong order.

A Blood leaves the left ventricle of the heart and flows to the body.

B Blood moves from the left atrium to the left ventricle.

C Blood moves from the right atrium to the right ventricle.

D Blood leaves the lungs and moves to the left atrium of the heart.

E Blood returns to the right atrium of the heart from the body.

F Blood leaves the right ventricle and moves to the lungs.

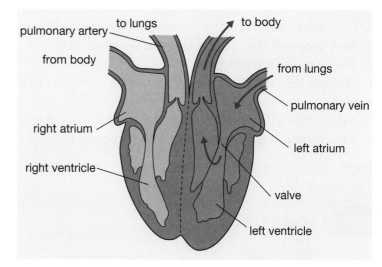

Arrange these sentences in the right order. Start with the letter **A**

A → ☐ → ☐ → ☐ → ☐ → ☐   [5 marks]

3. Blood picks up oxygen in the lungs and then returns to the heart. The oxygen is carried to the rest of the body.

Use coloured crayons to draw on the diagram of the heart in question 2:

a Use a **red** pencil to colour in the parts of the heart that contain oxygenated blood.   [1 mark]

b Use a **blue** pencil to add arrows showing the movement of blood through the **right** side of the heart.   [1 mark]

4. Red blood cells carry oxygen in the blood.

Red blood cells have a flattened disc shape instead of being like a ball.

Explain why this shape helps red blood cells carry as much oxygen as possible.

_____

_____

Support
You need to **explain why,** which means you have to link the shape of the cells to how the oxygen gets into them. Link by using 'this is because' or 'so that'.

_____

_____   [2 marks]

Heart problems

- Fatty material can build up in the coronary arteries. This means less oxygen gets to the heart muscle, so it cannot work very well. This is coronary heart disease (CHD).
- The fat contains cholesterol.
- CHD can be treated using stents to keep the arteries open or by taking statins to reduce cholesterol levels in the blood.
- Weak or leaky heart valves can be replaced with mechanical valves or transplanted valves (from humans or pigs).
- If the heart is too weak to pump blood properly, patients could have a heart transplant or an artificial heart.

1. What is a stent?

Tick **one** box.

☐ A part of the heart

☐ A device to hold a coronary artery open

☐ A mechanical heart valve   [1 mark]

2. Name **two** treatments for coronary heart disease.

1 _____

2 _____   [2 marks]

3. How can changing your diet help prevent coronary heart disease?

_____

_____   [1 mark]

4. Muscles need oxygen for them to work well.

Explain why narrowing of the coronary arteries causes heart disease.

build-up of fatty material

Support
Use the information you are given. Do not just repeat the information.

_____

_____

_____   [2 marks]

5. Treatments for coronary heart disease include taking drugs or inserting a mechanical device called a stent. Making a decision about treatment means considering the risks from an operation, the effects of drugs and possible failure of mechanical devices.

a Give **one** benefit and **one** risk for the patient of taking a drug for coronary heart disease instead of using a mechanical method.

Benefit _____

Risk _____ [2 marks]

b If the heart fails completely, a heart transplant may be considered.

Suggest **two** reasons why having a heart transplant is not more common.

> **Support**
> Think about what is needed for a heart transplant – a new heart (where does this come from?), surgery…

i _____

ii _____ [2 marks]

Risk factors for non-infectious diseases

- A non-infectious or non-communicable disease cannot be spread from person to person.
- Risk factors increase the chance of having a disease or affecting an unborn baby.
- Lifestyle such as poor diet, smoking and drinking alcohol are risk factors for coronary heart disease or type 2 diabetes.
- Smoking cigarettes is a risk factor for lung disease and lung cancer.
- Substances that increase the risk of cancer are called carcinogens. Carcinogens include ionising radiation.

1. Describe how a non-communicable disease is different from an infectious disease.

_____

_____ [1 mark]

2. Here are some possible risk factors for disease:

| Poor diet | Smoking | Viral infection | Obesity |

a Give **two** risk factors for cardiovascular disease.

i _____

ii _____ [2 marks]

b Give **two** risk factors for Type 2 diabetes.

i _____

ii _____ [2 marks]

3. When mothers drink too much alcohol during pregnancy, their babies may develop foetal alcohol syndrome (FAS). Many of the baby's organs are affected, including the brain, liver and kidneys.

The table below shows some information about FAS in the United States.

Year	Rate of FAS (number of cases reported per 10 000 births)
1979	1
1983	1.8
1987	2.1
1991	3.6

Support
'Per' means 'divided by'.
A rate of 1 per 10 000 means that 1 baby in every 10 000 born had FAS. Another way to write 1 per 10 000 is 1 / 10 000. In 1979 1 in 10 000 babies had FAS. In 1983 the rate was 1.8, which is equivalent to 18 babies per 100 000.

a Complete the bar chart using the information in the table.

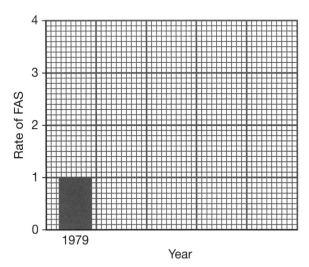

[2 marks]

b Describe the trend shown by this data.

_____

_____

Support
Describing a **trend** of a graph is describing the 'shape' of the graph.

[1 mark]

c In 1979, 3 000 000 babies were born in the United States.

Calculate how many babies had FAS.

Number of babies born with FAS = total number of babies born × rate of FAS in 1979

$$= 3\ 000\ 000 \times \frac{1}{10\ 000}$$

_____

Number of babies born with FAS = _____ [2 marks]

d In 1991, 4 000 000 babies were born in the United States.

Calculate how many babies had FAS.

_____

_____

_____

_____

_____

Number of babies born with FAS = _____ [2 marks]

Cancer

- Sometimes cells change so that they keep dividing uncontrollably.
- Too many new cells are produced, and a tumour forms.
- Benign tumours do not spread to other parts of the body.
- Malignant tumour cells are cancers. These cells spread to many parts of the body.
- Both our lifestyle and genetic risk factors can increase the risk of cancer.

1. What is the name given to substances that cause cancer?

_____ [1 mark]

2. Draw **one** line from each **word** to its correct **definition**.

Word	Definition
Malignant tumour	A slow-growing tumour, that does not spread to other body tissues
Cancerous	Cells become this when they start to divide uncontrollably
Benign tumour	A fast-growing tumour that can spread to other body tissues

[3 marks]

3. Some scientists carried out a study into the risk factors for lung cancer. They found that smoking tobacco, working in a dusty environment and a family history of cancers all increased the risk of lung cancer.

Before it was published, the work was looked at closely to see if the results were **valid**. The table below shows the findings. **Tick** the correct column for **each** finding. One has been done for you.

Support
Valid means you can trust the results to be correct.

Finding	Increases validity	Decreases validity
The study took place in only one hospital.		✓
The scientists compared patients with lung cancer to similar people without lung cancer (controls).		
The study was carried out with male and female patients.		
The study looked at fewer than 500 patients.		
Other scientists have found similar results.		

[4 marks]

4. Suggest **one** risk factor, other than smoking, for developing lung cancer.

_____

_____ [1 mark]

Looking at leaves

- The leaf is a plant organ that carries out photosynthesis.
- The leaf is made up of different tissues that have different jobs.
- These tissues include the epidermis, the palisade and spongy mesophyll, the xylem and phloem and the guard cells.
- The leaf has air spaces for diffusion of gases.

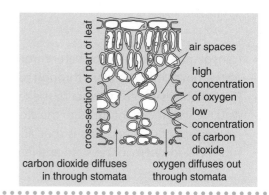

cross-section of part of leaf

air spaces

high concentration of oxygen

low concentration of carbon dioxide

carbon dioxide diffuses in through stomata

oxygen diffuses out through stomata

1. Where in a plant is photosynthesis carried out?

_____ [1 mark]

2. What is the name of the outer or surface layer of a leaf? Tick **one** box.

☐ Stoma ☐ Epidermis ☐ Chloroplast [1 mark]

3. The diagram shows a section through a leaf.

Use terms from the diagram to complete the sentences below. Each term may be used more than once.

The _____ or pore allows gases to diffuse in and out of the leaf.

The stoma is surrounded by two

_____.

The palisade cells are regular shaped cells packed together near the top of the cell. They contain many

_____. [3 marks]

upper epidermis

palisade cells

green chloroplasts

palisade layer

spongy mesophyll cell

spongy mesophyll layer

lower epidermis

guard cell   stoma (pore)   guard cell

Support
'Regular' means that the cells are the same shape and size.

4. Photosynthesis is carried out in the chloroplasts.

a Which cells in the leaf contain chloroplasts?

_____ [1 mark]

b Photosynthesis uses water and what gas? _____ [1 mark]

c How do gases enter and leave the leaf?

_____ [1 mark]

d What gas is produced during photosynthesis? _____ [1 mark]

Water movement in plants

- Transpiration is the flow of water through the plant.
- Water moves into the plant through root hair cells on the root.
- The xylem vessels carry water to the rest of the plant.
- Water leaves the plant through the stomata in the leaves.
- The surface of root hair cells is specialised to absorb water and minerals.
- Tubes called xylem in the stem and leaves are adapted to transport water.

1. Where does water enter the plant? _____ [1 mark]

2. Transpiration is the flow of water through a plant. The rate of transpiration depends on environmental factors.

Place a **tick** in either the 'increases' or 'decreases' transpiration rate column to show how each environmental factor affects the rate of transpiration.

Environmental factor	Increases transpiration rate	Decreases transpiration rate
Higher temperatures		
Higher humidity		
Higher light intensity		
Higher wind speed		

[4 marks]

3. The following statements describe the flow of water through a plant.

Use the letters to fill in the boxes below to put the statements in order. The first one has been done for you.

(A) Water moves across the root to enter the xylem by osmosis.

(B) Water moves up the root and stem in the xylem.

(C) Water diffuses out of the leaf.

(D) Water evaporates from the surface of the leaf cell.

(E) Water leaves the xylem and moves into the leaf.

(F) Water enters the root hair cell from the soil by osmosis.

F → ☐ → ☐ → ☐ → ☐ → ☐ [5 marks]

4. The root hair cell and the xylem are adapted to their function. Some adaptations are shown in the box.

Very thin cell wall   Thick waterproof cell wall   No cytoplasm Large surface area   Forms long tubes

Support
Think about what each cell type does – what does it need to perform its function?

(a) Which **two** of these adaptations are shown by xylem tissue?

i _____   ii _____ [2 mark]

(b) Which **two** of these adaptations are shown by the root hair cell?

i _____   ii _____ [2 mark]

Minerals and sugar movement in plants

- Water, minerals and food molecules move round the plant in the xylem and phloem.
- Water and minerals move up the plant through the xylem.
- Food molecules move from the leaves to the rest of the plant in the phloem. This is translocation.
- The xylem and phloem contain specialised cells that are adapted to their jobs.

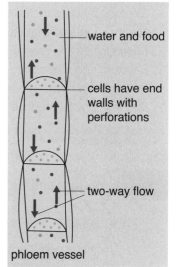

water and food

cells have end walls with perforations

two-way flow

phloem vessel

1. In a plant, water moves from the roots to the leaves. Why is it needed in the leaves?

_____ [1 mark]

2. Transpiration and translocation are two important transport processes in plants. The table below gives some details of the two processes.

	Transpiration	Translocation
Substance moved	water	food molecules
Cells used for transport	xylem	phloem
Direction of movement	from roots to leaves	from leaves to the rest of the plant

Compare transpiration and translocation.

Show Me

Transpiration and translocation are both forms of transport in plants.

However, translocation _____

but transpiration _____

_____

_____ [4 marks]

Support
Remember, a **compare** question means give similarities **and** differences. Good words to use in your answer are 'both', 'but' or 'however'. Remember, **4** marks means **four** comparisons are needed.

3. Minerals are carried through the plant dissolved in water.

Complete these sentences about the transport of water. Use words from the box.

Xylem	Phloem	Root hair

Minerals enter the root via the _____ cell. The _____ carries the minerals to the rest of the plant. [2 marks]

4. There is a higher concentration of minerals in the plant than in the soil.

What is the name of the process by which minerals are taken up into the plant?

_____ [1 mark]

5. Describe how phloem is specialised to allow substances to flow from one cell to the next.

_____

_____ [2 marks]

Microorganisms and disease

- Microorganisms include bacteria, protists, viruses and fungi.
- Microorganisms that cause disease are called pathogens.
- Microorganisms can cause disease in both plants and animals.
- Bacteria and viruses reproduce (increase in number) very quickly once inside the body.
- Bacteria may produce toxins (poisons) which make us ill.
- Viruses can only reproduce inside plant or animal cells and this damages the cells they are in.

1. Bacteria and viruses both cause disease. Complete the sentences to compare bacteria and viruses.

a Bacteria reproduce inside the body but viruses must

reproduce _____ [1 mark]

b Bacteria make us feel ill by producing _____. [1 mark]

c Viruses make us ill by damaging the _____ they have infected. [1 mark]

2. The table shows some human diseases. State whether each disease is caused by **bacteria** or a **virus**.

Disease	Caused by
Measles	
Salmonella food poisoning	
Gonorrhoea	
AIDS	

[4 marks]

3. Bacteria reproduce very quickly in the body. They divide in two by the process of mitosis. In warm conditions, with plenty of food, some bacteria can divide every 20 minutes.

a Starting with one bacterium, how many bacteria will be present after 1 hour?

After 20 minutes, number of bacteria = 1 × 2

After 40 minutes, number of bacteria = 1 × _____ × _____

1 hour is 60 minutes so after 1 hour,
number of bacteria = 1 × _____ × _____ ×

Number of bacteria = _____ [1 mark]

b Starting with one bacterium, how many bacteria will be present after 2 hours?

_____

_____

Number of bacteria = _____ [1 mark]

Spread of disease

- Microorganisms that cause disease are spread by contact, through food or water or through the air.
- Measles is spread by breathing in droplets from sneezes or coughs.
- *Salmonella* food poisoning is spread by eating contaminated food.
- HIV and gonorrhoea are spread by sexual contact. HIV is also spread in body fluids including blood.
- Malaria is spread by mosquito bites.

Contaminated food and water pass in through the mouth

Microorganisms in the air enter the nose

Microorganisms enter through the skin

Infected reproductive organs can pass on disease

1. Which of these diseases is spread through droplets in the air? Tick **one** box.

☐ HIV/AIDS

☐ Measles

☐ *Salmonella* food poisoning

[1 mark]

2. Suggest **one** way that food can become contaminated with *Salmonella* bacteria.

_____

_____ [2 marks]

Support
Food is **contaminated** when something that shouldn't be there has become mixed with it. This can include bacteria or viruses. You need to say **where** the *Salmonella* bacteria may be, and **how** they would get onto the food.

3. The table below shows some diseases. For each disease listed, place a **tick** in the correct column to show how each disease is spread.

Disease	How the disease is spread		
	Contact	Food or water	Air
Measles			
HIV			
Salmonella			
Gonorrhoea			

[4 marks]

4. HIV infection can lead to the development of AIDS if it is not treated. AIDS infections are often fatal.

The table below shows the number of new cases of HIV and the number of people dying from AIDS between 1995 and 2009 in the UK.

Year	New HIV infections	Deaths from AIDS
1995	2900	1700
1997	2800	746
1999	3200	470
2001	5100	470
2003	7300	573
2005	8000	590
2009	6600	510

Source – data modified from www.nhshistory.net/aidsdata.pdf

a Describe the trend in the number of new HIV infections between 1995 and 2005.

_____

_____ [2 marks]

Support
Remember, a **trend** is a pattern in data. There are **2 marks** so don't just say 'it goes up' or 'it goes down'. Compare the increase in each time period.

b Does the trend continue between 2005 and 2009?

_____ [1 mark]

c Calculate the percentage change in the number of deaths from AIDS between **1995** and **2005**. Use the equation below.

$$\text{percentage change} = \frac{\text{actual change}}{\text{original amount}} \times 100$$

Support
You need to know how to calculate a percentage change. The formula will not usually be given in the question.

_____

Show Me

Change in number of cases: 1700 – 590 = _____

$$\text{Percentage change} = \frac{}{1700} \times 100$$

_____

Percentage change = _____ %   [2 marks]

d Calculate the percentage change in the number of deaths from AIDS between **2005** and **2009**.

_____

_____

Percentage change = _____ %   [2 marks]

e Suggest a cause for the decrease in the number of new cases of HIV.

Support
A cause is the reason why something has happened.

_____

_____ [1 mark]

Malaria

- Malaria is a disease caused by a protist (a type of single-celled organism).
- This microorganism spends part of its life cycle in human blood.
- Malaria causes repeated fevers and can be fatal.
- Mosquitos are a vector for malaria. This means they spread the disease but do not cause it.
- Stopping mosquitos breeding and using mosquito nets helps control the spread of malaria.

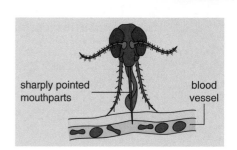

sharply pointed mouthparts   blood vessel

---

1. What type of organism causes malaria?
Tick **one** box.

☐ Bacteria   ☐ Fungus   ☐ Protist   ☐ Virus   [1 mark]

2. The malaria protist is a single-celled organism that lives for part of the time in human blood.

Put the following statements in order to show how someone can get infected with malaria. The first one is done for you.

A The protists reproduce again in the red blood cells. They leave the red blood cells and enter a new cell, causing further infection.

B The protist travels to the liver and reproduces.

C Blood from a person infected with the protist is sucked up by a feeding mosquito.

D The mosquito feeds on a healthy person and the protist is injected into them.

E The new protists leave the liver and enter red blood cells.

| C | → | ☐ | → | ☐ | → | ☐ | → | ☐ | [4 marks] |

3. In 2000, just over a million people (1 100 000) died of malaria. In 2015, only 440 000 people died.

> **Support**
> Remember, to calculate a percentage change, first calculate the change in the amount. Then divide by the original amount. Then multiply by 100 to convert the fraction into a percentage.

a Calculate the percentage decrease in the number of deaths between 2000 and 2015.

_____

_____

Percentage decrease = _____ %   [2 marks]

b About half the world's population is still at risk of malaria.

Female mosquitos lay their eggs in still water.

Explain why draining small ponds helps to reduce the number of cases of malaria.

Show Me   Fewer ponds so mosquitos _____

This means _____   [2 marks]

c Mosquitos mostly bite at night. Suggest how mosquito nets soaked in insecticide can help prevent malaria.

_____

_____

[2 marks]

Plant diseases

- Tobacco mosaic virus (TMV) affects many species of plants including tomatoes.
- The leaves become patchy in colour and the plant cannot photosynthesise very well.
- Rose black spot is a fungal disease that affects roses.
- Black spot can be treated with fungicide and by removing infected leaves.

1. State the reason why **fungicides** do not cure TMV.

_____ [1 mark]

2. Some facts about tobacco mosaic virus (TMV) infection in tomato plants are shown below. Draw **one** line from each fact to the correct explanation.

Fact		Explanation
The leaves on infected plants are patchy in colour pattern		because photosynthesis is reduced.
The infected plant cannot photosynthesise efficiently		because TMV kills small patches of cells and turns them white.
The plant does not grow well. Crop yields are smaller		because the leaves have many dead patches of cells.

[3 marks]

3. Gardeners try to treat black spot by spraying roses with fungicide. They also collect and burn infected leaves and branches.

Explain how these two methods help prevent the spread of black spot in the garden.

Spraying with fungicide: _____

_____

Removing and burning infected leaves and branches: _____

_____ [2 marks]

4. A gardener wants to see how effective his new fungicide is. He has two rose plants. He sprays one plant with fungicide every 2 weeks. He sprays the other plant with water. He records how many leaves on each plant develop black spots.

Suggest how he should make the test a fair comparison.

_____

_____

_____

Support
This question asks you to make suggestions. **3** marks means **three** ideas are needed. Your answers should link what you already know and the information in the question.

[3 marks]

Human defence systems

- Most microorganisms never enter very far into our bodies because our skin, breathing system and stomach all help to keep them out.
- The immune system also tries to destroy any microorganisms that manage to get inside our bodies.
- White blood cells are part of the immune system.
- Some white blood cells can surround and destroy microorganisms.
- Other white blood cells make chemicals called antibodies, which kill microorganisms or anti-toxins which remove toxins.

micro-organism

toxins

white blood cell

anti-toxins

1. What is the name of the substance in the stomach that kills bacteria?

_____ [1 mark]

2. When the skin is cut, a scab forms. How does this help prevent infection?

_____ [1 mark]

3. When you breathe in, the air you breathe can include particles containing microorganisms. How does the body prevent microorganisms getting into the lungs?

_____

_____ [2 marks]

4. White blood cells are part of the immune system. They defend the body against microorganisms that have managed to enter the body.

Describe **two** ways that white blood cells help to destroy microorganisms that have entered the body.

_____

_____ [2 marks]

Vaccination

- Vaccines can prevent infection.
- When many people are vaccinated, the spread of disease is reduced.
- Vaccines stimulate the immune system to make antibodies.
- Once a particular antibody is made, it can be made again easily.
- Vaccination means the body can quickly produce antibodies to the same pathogen that was in the vaccine.

1. What do vaccines cause the immune system to produce?

Tick **one** box.

☐ Antibodies   ☐ Antiseptic   ☐ Red blood cells   [1 mark]

2. The following steps explain how vaccination provides long-lasting protection against infections.

Put the sequence in order in the boxes below. The first step has been done for you.

A The antibodies kill the microorganism before it can cause disease.

B The body remembers the microorganism and quickly produces antibodies to it.

C A microorganism identical to the one in the vaccine enters the body some years later.

D The vaccine is injected into the body. It contains inactive or weakened microorganisms that will not cause illness.

E The vaccine causes the white blood cells to produce antibodies.

D → ☐ → ☐ → ☐ → ☐   [4 marks]

3. The measles vaccine was introduced in 1968.

The table shows the number of cases of measles and the number of measles deaths in the UK after the introduction of the vaccine.

Year	Number of measles cases	Number of measles deaths
1970	307 408	42
1980	139 487	26
1990	13 302	1
2000	2378	1
2010	2235	0

a How did the number of cases of and deaths from measles change between 1970 and 2010?

_____ [1 mark]

b Compare how the numbers of cases changed from 1970 to 1980 with 1980 to 1990.

_____

_____

[2 marks]

Support
Remember, in compare questions you need to look for similarities or differences. Use data from the table.

c If most people have been vaccinated against measles, other people who have not been vaccinated have a low risk of catching measles. Complete the sentences below to explain why.

When most of the population is vaccinated, the number of people catching the disease

_____.

Most people are immune to measles so the spread of the disease from an infected person

_____.

Unvaccinated children are _____ likely to come into contact with anyone who has measles.

[3 marks]

Bacteria and antibiotics

- Antibiotics are drugs that kill bacteria inside the body.
- Antibiotics have greatly reduced the number of deaths caused by bacterial infections.
- Antibiotics do not work against viruses.
- Bacteria are becoming resistant to antibiotics; it takes time to develop new antibiotics that work against the drug-resistant bacteria.
- Painkillers can be used to treat the symptoms of infection but they do not cure it.

1. The common cold is caused by a virus. Answer these questions about getting a cold.

a Why will antibiotics **not** help if you feel ill from a cold?

_____ [1 mark]

b A cold may give you a high temperature and a headache.

What type of drug should you use to treat these symptoms?

_____ [1 mark]

2. Tuberculosis (TB) is an infection caused by a bacterium. The table below shows the number of cases of TB in the UK since 1913.

Year	Number of cases of TB
1913	117 000
1987	5 000
2000	6 300
2011	8 700

a The number of cases of TB decreased sharply between 1913 and 1987.

Give **two** reasons for the decrease.

i _____

ii _____ [2 marks]

b TB infections were lowest in 1987. After this the number of cases started to **increase**. Calculate the percentage increase from 1987 to 2011.

_____

_____

> **Support**
> Remember, to calculate a percentage change, first find the change in the amount. Then divide by the original amount. Then multiply by 100 to convert the fraction into a percentage.

Percentage increase = _____ % [2 marks]

3. Recently there has been an increase in the number of TB cases worldwide. One of the reasons for the increase is that some cases of TB cannot be treated.

a Why can some cases of TB not be treated?

_____ [1 mark]

b It takes a long time to develop new antibiotics. Suggest **two** ways that we can make sure our existing antibiotics remain effective against serious diseases like TB.

_____

_____ [2 marks]

Making and testing new drugs

- Some older drugs were extracted from plants and microorganisms.
- Examples are digitalis, aspirin and penicillin.
- Newer drugs are completely human-made, or based on substances found in plants.
- Before use, drugs must be tested to see if they work and if they have any side effects.
- In clinical trials some patients get a placebo. This does not contain any of the drug being tested.

1. Draw **one** line from each of the drugs below to its source.

Aspirin		*Penicillium* mould
Digitalis		Foxgloves
Penicillin		Willow trees

[3 marks]

2. Before a new drug can be used it must be tested to make sure it is **effective** and **safe**. Complete the sentences to explain what is meant by these words.

a Effective means that the new drug will prevent or _____ the disease.

b Safe means that there are not too many _____. [2 marks]

3. When a drug is being tested and trialled, some people are given the drug and some are given a **placebo**. The people in the trial do not know whether they are taking the drug or the placebo.

What is the purpose of including a placebo in drug trials? Tick **one** box.

☐ To make sure there are no side effects

☐ To act as a control group to compare the effects of the drug

☐ To make the drug appear more effective than it is [1 mark]

4. There are several stages of testing and trialling a drug. These are shown in order below.

A Preclinical tests; no human patients

B Clinical trials, stage 1

C Clinical trials, stage 2

D Clinical trials, stage 3

Write the letter of the stage where these activities occur.

One hundred to 300 patients are given the drug to see if it works. _____ [1 mark]

A few healthy people take the drug to make sure it is safe. _____ [1 mark]

Many patients take the drug over a long time to look for rare side effects. _____ [1 mark]

The drug is tested on cells and tissues in the laboratory. _____ [1 mark]

Photosynthesis for food

- Photosynthesis is the process plants use to make food.
- All other living things use the food made by plants.
- Glucose is produced by photosynthesis.
- The plant can turn the glucose into all the other substances it needs.
- To produce proteins, nitrates must be added to the glucose – the nitrates come from the soil.

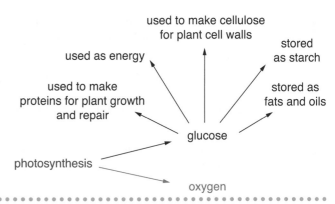

1. Photosynthesis makes glucose and what other product?

_____ [1 mark]

2. Food chains and webs can be used to look at feeding relationships between living things.

a A simple food chain is shown below. Why does the arrow point from grass to cow?

Grass ➡ Cow ➡ Human

_____ [1 mark]

b Why are plants such as grass called producers?

_____ [1 mark]

c Why are animals such as cows called consumers?

_____ [1 mark]

3. Glucose is made during photosynthesis. It is used in many ways by the plant.

a Some glucose is used to provide the cells with energy. What is the name of the chemical reaction that releases the energy stored in glucose?

_____ [1 mark]

b Some glucose is stored for future use inside the plant cells. What is the name of the carbohydrate molecule that is used for storage?

_____ [1 mark]

c Plant cell walls are made from a different carbohydrate molecule. What is the name of this molecule?

_____ [1 mark]

4. Which two chemicals are linked together to produce the small molecules that make proteins?

_____ and _____ [2 marks]

Photosynthesis equation

- A plant needs carbon dioxide and water to carry out photosynthesis.
- The products of photosynthesis are oxygen and glucose.
- Energy from sunlight is used to make the reaction work.
- The energy is captured by chlorophyll.
- The photosynthesis reaction can be written as a word equation.

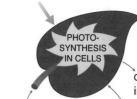

light from Sun

PHOTO-
SYNTHESIS
IN CELLS

oxygen released
into the air

water from soil
taken in

carbon dioxide enters
the leaf from the air

---

1. The word equation for photosynthesis is shown below. Fill in the missing word.

Carbon dioxide + water $\xrightarrow{\text{Light}}$ _____ + oxygen

[1 mark]

Support
Light is written over the arrow because it is needed for photosynthesis but it is not a chemical that takes part in the reaction.

2. The chemicals involved in photosynthesis are shown below. Draw **one** line from each chemical name to its matching formula.

Carbon dioxide		H_2O
Water		$C_6H_{12}O_6$
Glucose		O_2
Oxygen		CO_2

Support
The small subscript numbers tell you how many atoms of each element are in the molecule. H is the symbol for hydrogen, C is for carbon and O is for oxygen.

[4 marks]

3. To carry out photosynthesis, the plant needs energy.

a Which green pigment absorbs light energy?

_____ [1 mark]

b Photosynthesis is a chemical reaction that takes in energy from the surroundings. Which of these words means a chemical reaction that **takes in** energy? Tick **one** box.

Exothermic ☐ Endothermic ☐

Support
Remember that <u>ex</u>it means going out.

[1 mark]

4. Write the correct words in the sentences below.

Some plant cells contain small cell parts called _____.
These carry out photosynthesis.

The green parts of plants contain a green pigment called

_____.

This captures the light energy for photosynthesis. [2 marks]

Support
It is important to spell some words very carefully as they look similar. **Chlorophyll** and **chloroplasts** are two photosynthesis key words that look similar but have different meanings.

Factors affecting photosynthesis

- The rate of photosynthesis is how fast photosynthesis takes place.
- Light intensity, temperature and amount of carbon dioxide affect the rate of photosynthesis.
- The rate of photosynthesis is often investigated using pondweed; pondweed is aquatic (lives in water).

 1. Photosynthesis is faster when the light intensity and temperature are higher.

Circle the correct word in **bold** in these sentences about photosynthesis.

The rate of photosynthesis is **higher/lower** at midday than earlier in the day. [1 mark]

In the tropics the temperature is **higher/lower** than in Europe, so the rate of photosynthesis is higher. [1 mark]

 2. A student is designing an experiment to look at the effect of increasing light intensity on the rate of photosynthesis. This is a list of the equipment and materials they used.

- lamp
- large beaker filled with water
- metre ruler
- test tube
- pondweed
- timer

a When the pondweed is placed in water you can see the bubbles of oxygen made by photosynthesis.

How will the student measure how quickly the pondweed is photosynthesising?

_____

_____ [2 marks]

b The lamp will be used as the light source. The student placed the lamp at different distances from the pondweed.

Suggest the range of values the student should use.

_____ [1 mark]

> **Support**
> A range sometimes means the highest number minus the lowest number. Here, you are asked to state the smallest and the largest measurements to be used.

c It is important to control key variables to make a fair test. The student places the pondweed in a test tube of water and then places the test tube in the beaker of water.

Which factor is the student trying to control?

_____ [1 mark]

3. The student repeated the experiment four times, counting the number of bubbles each time. The results were recorded in a table.

The mean number of bubbles given off in 5 minutes was calculated for each distance from the lamp using the equation

$$\text{mean} = \frac{(\text{Count 1} + \text{Count 2} + \text{Count 3} + \text{Count 4})}{4}$$

a Calculate the rate of photosynthesis using the equation below. The first one has been done for you.

$$\text{Rate of photosynthesis} = \frac{\text{mean number of bubbles counted}}{\text{time bubbles counted}}$$

Distance of lamp from pondweed (m)	Number of bubbles counted in 5 minutes				Mean number of bubbles	Rate of photosynthesis $\left(\frac{\text{bubbles}}{\text{min}}\right)$
	Count 1	Count 2	Count 3	Count 4		
0.1	10	9	11	10	10.0	$\frac{10.0}{5} = 2$
0.2	7	5	5	6	5.75	
0.3	3	4	3	2	3.0	
0.4	2	1	1	2	1.5	
0.5	1	0	1	0	0.5	

[4 marks]

b Plot a scatter graph of the results. Place the light intensity on the x-axis and the rate of photosynthesis on the y-axis. Remember to label the axes clearly, including the units. Draw a curved line of best fit. [4 marks]

Support
The x-axis is a bit tricky in this experiment. Remember to go up in even steps of light intensity, e.g. 2, 4, 6, 8, 10.

c What conclusion can be made as the distance from the lamp increases?

_____ [1 mark]

d Use your graph to read off the rate of photosynthesis at a distance of 0.15 m.

Rate = _____ bubbles / min   [1 mark]

Cell respiration

- Cells gain their energy in a chemical reaction called respiration.
- The reaction takes place in the mitochondria of the cell.
- The reaction releases the energy stored in glucose, and produces carbon dioxide and water.
- Aerobic respiration requires oxygen.
- The respiration reaction can be written as a word equation.
- Respiration and other metabolic reactions are controlled by enzymes.

1. All cells respire, all the time. Where in the cell does respiration take place?

Tick **one** box.

☐ Nucleus   ☐ Mitochondria   ☐ Cell membrane   [1 mark]

2.

a Complete the word equation for aerobic respiration.

Glucose + _____ → _____ + _____ [3 marks]

b Which of the substances involved in respiration are:

i the reactants?

_____ and _____ [1 mark]

ii the products?

_____ and _____ [1 mark]

3. All organisms need energy for their living processes. Some energy is needed for metabolic reactions, such as building new molecules and breaking down waste substances. Give **two** other ways your body uses energy from respiration.

1 _____

2 _____ [2 marks]

4. Draw **one** line from each chemical involved in respiration to its matching formula.

Oxygen		H_2O
Carbon dioxide		$C_6H_{12}O_6$
Glucose		O_2
Water		CO_2

[4 marks]

5. Respiration is a reaction that gives out energy.

What is the name for a chemical reaction that **gives out** energy?

_____ [1 mark]

Anaerobic respiration

- Anaerobic respiration does not require oxygen.
- We use yeast cells respiring anaerobically to make bread and alcoholic drinks.

· ·

1. What is the name for the type of respiration that requires oxygen?

_____ [1 mark]

2. For at least a short time, cells can survive without oxygen. But they must still carry out respiration, to provide the energy they need to survive. What is the name for the type of respiration that does **not** require oxygen?

_____ [1 mark]

3. Yeast cells can use anaerobic respiration to provide the energy they need.

a Complete the word equation for anaerobic respiration in yeast cells.

_____ ➡ ethanol + _____ [2 marks]

b Yeast is used to make bread. Which of the products of anaerobic respiration (fermentation) becomes trapped in small pockets in the bread dough, helping the bread to rise?

_____ [1 mark]

c Which of the products of fermentation is helpful in the making of wine?

_____ [1 mark]

4. The equation for aerobic respiration is shown below. Compare aerobic and anaerobic respiration in yeast cells.

Glucose + oxygen ➡ carbon dioxide + water

_____

_____

_____ [3 marks]

5. A student carried out an experiment to investigate the effect of temperature on the rising of bread dough.

They put the same amount of dough into six different measuring cylinders. Each cylinder was placed in a separate water bath. Each water bath was at a different temperature.

The volume of dough was measured after 1 hour. The results are shown in the table. Complete the sentences to explain the differences in the data.

Temperature (°C)	Change in volume of bread dough (cm³)
25	19
35	27
45	13
55	9

The fermentation of yeast produces the gas _____.

The amount of gas produced is maximum at a temperature of _____ °C. This means that the rate of respiration is maximum at this temperature.

The rate of respiration decreases at higher temperatures because reactions inside living cells are

controlled by _____. [3 marks]

Effect of exercise

- Muscle cells respire faster when we exercise as they need more energy.
- The heart rate, breathing rate and breathing volume all increase during exercise to provide the extra oxygen needed in the muscles.
- During intense exercise, muscle cells use oxygen faster than it can be provided.
- The cells start to respire anaerobically, producing lactic acid.
- High levels of lactic acid cause the muscles to become tired and stop working properly.
- Anaerobic respiration produces much less energy than aerobic respiration.

1. Write the word equation for anaerobic respiration in muscle cells.

_____ ➡ _____   [1 mark]

2. The key words for anaerobic respiration are shown below. Draw **one** line from each word to its correct definition.

Anaerobic respiration		The only product of anaerobic respiration in muscle cells
Glucose		Respiration without oxygen
Lactic acid		The only reactant needed for anaerobic respiration

[3 marks]

3. During exercise the muscle cells require more energy. To produce more energy, they must respire faster.

a The cells will need more oxygen and glucose. How are these substances carried to muscle cells?

_____   [1 mark]

b Why does the heart beat faster during exercise?

_____   [1 mark]

c Why does the breathing rate and depth of breathing increase during exercise?

_____   [1 mark]

4. During intense exercise the body cannot keep up with the need for oxygen in muscle cells. The muscle cells switch to anaerobic respiration.

Give **two** reasons why muscles cannot use **only** anaerobic respiration.

i. _____   [1 mark]

ii. _____   [1 mark]

Homeostasis

- The concentration of glucose in the blood, body temperature and water levels are examples of conditions inside the body that must be controlled.
- These controlled conditions are important for cells to function.
- Keeping these important conditions within normal levels is called homeostasis.
- Control systems automatically monitor and react to changes in body conditions to restore normal levels.

RECEPTOR CELLS detect changes in the environment → message → COORDINATOR receives and processes information → message → EFFECTOR muscles contracting or glands releasing hormones into the blood

1. State **two** substances that the body must keep the same inside the blood.

1 _____ [1 mark]

2 _____ [1 mark]

2. Match the key words to their definitions to show how the body monitors and reacts to changes in body conditions. Draw **one** line from each key word to its matching definition.

receptors		Receives and processes information about the change and brings about the response
coordinator		Muscles or glands that respond to the changes
effectors		Cells that sense changes in internal body conditions

[3 marks]

3. Complete the sentences below using words from the box.

| Body temperature   Glucose   Carbon dioxide   Water |

Support
In questions like this you may not need to use all the words. Sometimes you may need to use the same word twice.

When an athlete runs, their muscles use _____ to provide the energy for movement.

The athlete's hard-working muscles become hotter and so their _____ increases.

The athlete will sweat to cool down and so their body will lose _____. [3 marks]

4. Give **two** examples of organs in the body that respond to changes in the environment and act as **effectors**.

1 _____ [1 mark]

2 _____ [1 mark]

The nervous system and reflexes

- The nervous system allows us to detect and react to internal and external changes.
- The central nervous system (CNS) is the brain and spinal cord.
- Cells called neurones carry messages to and from the CNS as electrical impulses.
- Sensory neurones are found in receptors.
- Motor neurones end at an effector (a muscle or gland).
- It takes some time for information to move from the stimulus through the brain to bring about the response. This is the reaction time.
- Reflex actions are faster, automatic reactions that protect the body from danger. They happen faster because the information takes a short cut.

1. Put the words below into the right order in the boxes to show how the CNS responds to a stimulus.

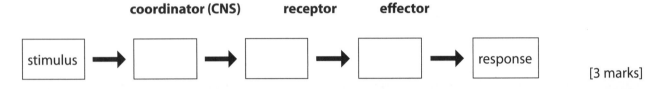

coordinator (CNS)   **receptor**   **effector**

stimulus ➡ ⬚ ➡ ⬚ ➡ ⬚ ➡ response

[3 marks]

2. You can measure your reaction time by trying to catch a falling ruler. Some students carried out a test to see if their reaction times were affected by whether they were distracted by noise. The results are shown in the table.

Gender	Mean reaction time (s)	
	With noise	**Without noise**
Girls	0.40	0.30
Boys	0.41	0.29

a Draw a bar chart of the results.   [2 marks]

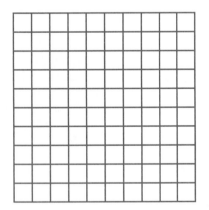

Support
There are two different ways you could draw the bars: both 'boys results' then 'both girls', or both 'with noise' results and then both 'without noise' results. It does not matter which you choose, but you must put the bars in an order that makes sense.

b Give **two** conclusions that can be made from your bar chart.

i _____   [1 mark]

ii _____   [1 mark]

Support
Compare the information. Talk about similarities or differences between the groups shown. Use data and numbers from the bar chart.

3. Imagine you accidentally put your hand in a flame. Your arm muscle will remove your hand very quickly to prevent it from being burned.

a Where are the cells that are acting as receptors in this reflex action?

_____ [1 mark]

b Which type of neurone connects the receptor to the central nervous system?

_____ [1 mark]

c In a reflex action, a relay neurone inside the spinal cord connects the sensory neurone straight to a motor neurone.

Explain why a reflex action is faster than a normal response to a stimulus.

_____

_____ [1 mark]

Support
This question asks you to **explain why**. This often means you should link ideas together using the word 'because'.

Hormones

- Hormones are chemicals that control some processes in the body, including the concentration of glucose in our blood.
- Hormones are made and secreted (given out) into the blood by specialised organs called glands.
- All the endocrine glands together make up the endocrine system.
- The pituitary gland releases hormones that control many of the other glands of the endocrine system.

1. How do hormones move from where they are made to their target organ?

_____ [1 mark]

2. Draw **one** line from each key word to its matching definition.

| endocrine system | A chemical messenger transported in the blood |

| endocrine glands | The group of glands that controls the body, using hormones |

| hormone | Glands that make hormones and release them into the blood |

[3 marks]

3. Use the words from the box below to label the diagram showing the organs of the endocrine system.

| Testes | Ovaries | Adrenal glands | Pituitary gland | Pancreas | Thyroid gland |

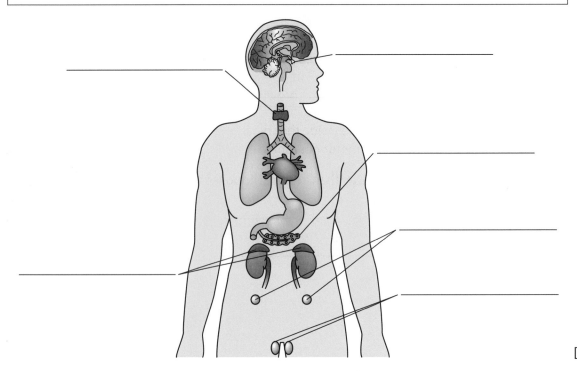

[6 marks]

4. **a** Which of these glands is **not** present in women?

_____ [1 mark]

b Which of these glands is **not** present in men?

_____ [1 mark]

Controlling blood glucose

- Blood glucose concentration is monitored and controlled by the pancreas.
- The pancreas releases the hormone insulin when blood glucose levels are too high.
- Insulin causes the liver to take glucose from the blood and store it as glycogen.
- In Type 1 diabetes, the pancreas does not make enough insulin.
- In Type 2 diabetes, the body no longer responds to insulin.
- Type 1 diabetes is treated with insulin injections.
- Type 2 diabetes cannot be treated with insulin, so exercise and avoiding sugary foods are important to keep glucose levels within safe limits.

1. If you cannot make insulin, what illness do you have?

_____ [1 mark]

2. It is important that there is the correct concentration of glucose in the blood.

a Which endocrine gland controls the concentration of glucose in the blood?

_____ [1 mark]

b Which hormone is released when blood glucose levels are too high?

_____ [1 mark]

c Which organ removes glucose from the blood when glucose levels are very high?

_____ [1 mark]

3. Two people were tested for their body's ability to control the amount of blood glucose. Both were given a glucose drink at the start of the experiment. The amount of glucose in their blood was measured for the next 150 minutes.

The graph shows the results of the test for both people. One person has diabetes. The other person does not.

a Complete the sentences to explain how the blood glucose concentration changes for the healthy person.

For the first 35 minutes, the concentration of blood glucose _____.

This is because the glucose is entering the _____ from the stomach.

After 35 minutes the concentration of blood glucose _____. This is

because the _____ has released insulin, and the _____ is removing

glucose from the blood. [5 marks]

b Compare the information shown in the graph for the healthy person and the person with diabetes.

_____

_____ [2 marks]

Support
Words ending in -er (e.g. greater, longer, hotter, heavier) are useful to compare two sets of information. Remember, **2** marks means you must make **two** points.

4. Explain why Type 2 diabetes cannot be controlled with insulin injections.

_____ [1 mark]

Hormones and puberty

- Certain hormones cause changes during puberty.
- The main female reproductive hormone is oestrogen.
- The female reproductive hormones cause women to start ovulation (releasing eggs) and have a menstrual cycle.
- The main male reproductive hormone is testosterone. It causes men to begin to produce sperm.
- These hormones cause body changes such as growing breasts (girls) or a moustache and beard (boys).
- These changes are the secondary sexual characteristics.

1. At what stage in your life does your body start to make reproductive hormones?

_____ [1 mark]

2. Complete these sentences about the hormones oestrogen and testosterone.

a Oestrogen is the _____ reproductive hormone; it is made in the

_____.

[2 marks]

b Testosterone is the _____ reproductive hormone; it is made in the

_____.

[2 marks]

3. Testosterone causes the male secondary characteristics to develop, such as growing hair on the face.

a State **two** other **secondary sexual characteristics** that are caused by testosterone.

i _____ [1 mark]

ii _____ [1 mark]

b What other major function does testosterone have?

_____ [1 mark]

4. The sentences below describe the stages of the menstrual cycle. Place the letters in the boxes below to give the correct sequence. The first one has been done for you.

A Ovulation occurs. The egg is released into the oviduct.

B If the egg is not fertilised, it dies and passes out of the vagina.

C The uterus lining that developed during the previous cycle is shed.

D A new egg starts to develop in the ovary and the uterus lining starts to grow again.

E The egg moves along the oviduct and the uterus lining is maintained.

| C | → | | → | | → | | → | |

[4 marks]

5. Oestrogen causes the uterus lining to thicken. In which stage of the menstrual cycle will this hormone be active? Give the letter of the correct stage from the sentences in question 4.

_____ [1 mark]

Hormones and the menstrual cycle

- The menstrual cycle is a 28-day cycle that occurs in women.
- During the cycle, an egg matures and is released. Also, the uterus (womb) is prepared to receive a fertilised egg.
- The cycle is controlled by four hormones, oestrogen, progesterone, FSH and LH.

1. How long is the menstrual cycle?

_____ [1 mark]

2. Draw **one** line from each key word to its definition.

menstrual cycle		The lining of the uterus comes off from about day 1 to day 5 of the menstrual cycle
menstruation (or period)		The reproductive cycle in women, usually lasting about 28 days
ovulation		The release of an egg from the ovary on about day 14 of the menstrual cycle

[3 marks]

3. Four hormones play an important part in the menstrual cycle. Complete the sentences to describe the role of each hormone.

Follicle stimulating hormone, or FSH, causes an _____ to mature in the ovaries.

Luteinising hormone, or LH, causes the _____ of an egg from the ovary.

Oestrogen and _____ prepare the lining of the uterus for pregnancy.

[3 marks]

4. The amounts of each female reproductive hormone in the blood change over the 28 days of the menstrual cycle. The graph shows how the levels of oestrogen and progesterone change during one woman's cycle.

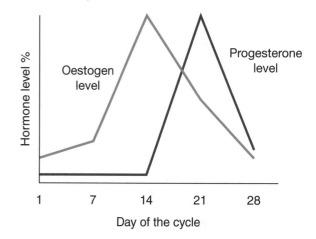

Ovulation occurs at about day 14. Draw a vertical line on the graph on this day and label it 'ovulation'.

[1 mark]

5. Use the graph from question 4 to answer these questions.

a Which hormone is at its highest level at ovulation? _____ [1 mark]

b When are both hormones at their lowest levels? _____ [1 mark]

c What else is happening in the menstrual cycle when both hormones are at their lowest levels?

_____ [1 mark]

Contraception

- Fertility (a man or woman's ability to have children) can be controlled to prevent pregnancy.
- Hormone pills, injections or skin patches can be used to stop the release of an egg in women.
- Other methods of contraception include barrier methods, spermicides, intra-uterine devices (IUDs) and natural planning.
- Both men and women can have sterilisation operations to prevent pregnancy permanently.

1. What word is used to describe the ability to produce children?

_____ [1 mark]

2. Many women use hormonal contraceptives (the Pill) to control fertility. However, there may be times when these methods are unsuitable. Some other methods of contraception are shown below.

Draw **one** line from each method of contraception to its matching explanation.

| condom | | The man and woman avoid sexual intercourse around the time of ovulation |

| natural planning or the safe period | | This prevents the sperm reaching the egg |

| IUD | | This is placed in the uterus (womb) to prevent the egg from implanting |

[3 marks]

3. When used carefully, condoms and the IUD are very effective at preventing pregnancy.

a Suggest why the natural planning method might be **less** effective.

_____ [1 mark]

b Women can use a spermicide together with a barrier method of contraception. What does a spermicide do?

_____ [1 mark]

c Surgical methods can also prevent pregnancy. In women the oviduct is cut; in men the sperm ducts are cut.

What is the main **disadvantage** of this type of contraception?

_____ [1 mark]

4. Sometimes hormonal contraceptives are given as an implant, injection or skin patch. The hormones are released slowly over a long period of time.

Suggest why this method might be more successful than taking hormonal contraceptives as a pill.

Support
When the question asks you to **suggest**, you must think about what you already know and come up with your own ideas about the new information you are given.

_____ [1 mark]

5. The table below compares the advantages and disadvantages of using oral contraceptives and condoms for contraception.

Use the information in the table to evaluate which form of contraception is the best for a sexually active young couple.

Contraceptive method	Advantages	Disadvantages
Contraceptive pill	• Very effective • Very convenient • May reduce risk of some cancers • Periods may be more regular and lighter	• Must be taken regularly • Sickness and diarrhoea will reduce effectiveness • Will not protect against sexually transmitted diseases • Only available from clinics and doctors • The combined pill is not suitable for older women or those with high blood pressure
Condoms	• Widely available • Effective if used properly • Can protect against sexually transmitted diseases • No health risks	• May slip off or split during intercourse • Must be withdrawn after ejaculation so as not to spill semen

Support
Do not simply write out information that is already in the question. You need to give a conclusion, with a reason.

You also need to link your sentences together in a sensible order to get full marks.

Useful words and phrases include 'however', 'but' and 'on the other hand'.

Support
You have to judge which method of contraception is the best for the couple. You have to give reasons for your choice using the information in the table.

_____

_____

_____

_____

_____

_____

_____

_____

_____

_____

_____

[6 marks]

Sexual reproduction and fertilisation

- In sexual reproduction two sex cells called gametes fuse (join).
- This is called fertilisation.
- One gamete comes from each parent.
- The gametes in animals are the sperm and egg cells.
- The gametes in flowering plants are pollen and egg cells.
- The fertilised egg has a mixture of chromosomes from both parents.
- This means the new individuals produced by sexual reproduction are all different from each other.

1. Give the name for these gametes.

Male gamete in animals _____ [1 mark]

Male gamete in flowering plants _____ [1 mark]

Female gamete in both animals and flowering plants _____ [1 mark]

2. **a** Gametes are produced from cells in the reproductive organs.

Name the organ where the male gamete is produced in animals.

_____ [1 mark]

b Name the organ where the female gamete is produced in animals.

_____ [1 mark]

3. **a** What is the name given to the process when a male and a female gamete fuse?

_____ [1 mark]

b Which statement correctly describes the chromosomes in the cell produced by sexual reproduction?

Tick **one** box.

☐ The cell contains chromosomes from the mother only

☐ The cell contains chromosomes from the father only

☐ The cell contains chromosomes from the father and the mother [1 mark]

c At fertilisation the two gametes join together to make a new cell.

Describe how this single, unspecialised cell changes to become an embryo with many different cells.

Support
This is another example of a question where you need to link knowledge. Think about what you know about cell division.

_____

_____

_____ [2 marks]

58

Asexual reproduction

- Asexual reproduction does not involve gametes.
- Asexual reproduction needs only one parent.
- The new organisms produced by asexual reproduction are all genetically identical and are called clones.

1. Name the type of reproduction in which clones are produced.

_____ [1 mark]

2. Name the type of reproduction that involves male and female gametes.

_____ [1 mark]

3. Strawberry plants produce horizontal stems called runners. A new plant develops at the end of the runner. This is an example of asexual reproduction.

Place **one** tick in the correct box to describe the genetic material of the new plant.

☐ The new plant is genetically identical to the parent but different from new plants on other runners from the same plant.

☐ The new plant is genetically different from the parent and different from new plants on other runners from the same plant.

☐ The new plant is genetically identical to the parent and the new plants on other runners from the same plant. [1 mark]

4. Complete the table below to compare sexual and asexual reproduction.

Support
Vocabulary: offspring means the person, animal or plant produced.

	Sexual reproduction	Asexual reproduction
Number of parents		
Are gametes involved?		
Are the offspring all different from the parents?		

[3 marks]

5. Complete the sentences to explain why the new individuals produced in asexual reproduction are genetically identical to the parent and to each other.

In asexual reproduction some of the parent's cells divide to form new cells that contain exactly the same

_____ as the parent cell.

This type of cell division is called _____. [2 marks]

Cell division by meiosis

- Meiosis is the type of cell division used to form sex cells (gametes).
- The cells formed by meiosis are not genetically identical.
- Gametes have half the normal number of chromosomes.
- When two gametes join the new cell has the normal number of chromosomes.

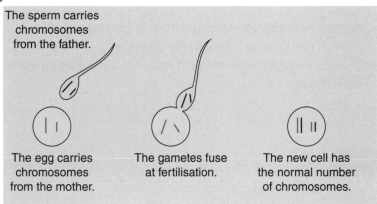

The sperm carries chromosomes from the father.

The egg carries chromosomes from the mother.

The gametes fuse at fertilisation.

The new cell has the normal number of chromosomes.

1. Sexual reproduction requires cells called **gametes**. Name the type of cell division that produces gametes.

_____ [1 mark]

2. A skin cell from a human contains 23 pairs of chromosomes, or a total of 46. How many chromosomes would you expect to find in a human sperm or egg cell?

_____ [1 mark]

3. Meiosis is the type of cell division that produces eggs and sperm. During meiosis, the cell divides once and then the two new cells divide again.

How many cells are formed during meiosis?

_____ [1 mark]

4. Complete the table below to show how the number of chromosomes in a human cell varies during sexual reproduction. The first one has been done for you.

Stage	Number of chromosomes per cell
Gamete formed in ovary or testes	23
Fertilisation – the egg and sperm fuse	
The fertilised cell divides by mitosis to form the embryo	

[2 marks]

5. Complete the sentences to explain how non-identical cells are formed by meiosis.

In normal human body cells there are pairs of chromosomes. One of each pair comes from the person's

father and one comes from the person's _____.

In the testes and ovaries, cells divide to produce sperms and eggs. This process is called

_____.

Each gamete now has only one _____ from each pair.

The chromosome of the pair that is included in a gamete is random. There are many millions of combinations that can be formed from 23 pairs of chromosomes.

This means that it is very unlikely that two gametes will be genetically _____. [4 marks]

Chromosomes and genes

- A DNA molecule has two spirals (helixes) coiled together.
- A gene is a small section of a DNA molecule.
- Each chromosome contains large numbers of genes.
- Chromosomes are in the nucleus.
- The genome of an organism is the entire genetic material of that organism.

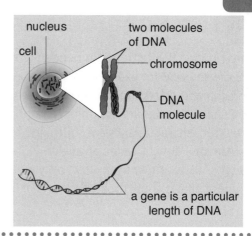

1. Draw **one** line from each word to match it to its definition.

gene		A molecule that has a structure of two strands arranged in a double helix
chromosome		A structure found in the nucleus of a cell that contains DNA
DNA		A short section of DNA

[3 marks]

2. What is the name for the entire genetic material of an organism?

Tick **one** box.

☐ a clone   ☐ a gamete   ☐ a gene   ☐ a genome   [1 mark]

3. The whole human genome is being studied by scientists to find out more about some human diseases. They have found genes that are linked to some types of cancer. Inheriting a certain gene means it can increase the risk of developing this type of cancer.

   a Which statement is correct? Tick **one** box.

   ☐ Cancer is an inherited disease.

   ☐ There are genetic risk factors for some types of cancer.

   ☐ Cancer is caused only by factors in the environment.   [1 mark]

   b Suggest one reason why it might be helpful for someone to know that they carry a gene for an increased risk of breast cancer.

   _____

[1 mark]

> **Support**
> In the final exam some of the marks will be for connecting your knowledge from different areas of biology. To answer this question you need to link knowledge of genes with ideas from an earlier topic about risk factors.

Inherited characteristics

- Genes provide the instructions needed to make proteins. Proteins are used to build different parts of the body, for example to make eyes blue or brown.
- Some characteristics show up in our appearance (our phenotype) but some do not.
- Some characteristics are controlled by only one gene.
- More often, characteristics are controlled by many genes working together.
- A version of a gene is called an allele.
- Recessive alleles show their effect only if both chromosomes have this allele.
- Dominant alleles show their effect even if only one chromosome has this allele.

1. Complete the sentences below.

The code for a single characteristic of an organism is contained in a _____. [1 mark]

Different versions of a gene are called _____. [1 mark]

2. Our cells have two copies of each gene. The alleles (or versions of the gene) can be the same or different for the two copies.

Complete the sentences.

a If a person is **homozygous** for a gene, both alleles

are _____. [1 mark]

b If a person is **heterozygous** for a gene, the alleles are _____. [1 mark]

> **Support**
> **Homo-** is often added to the start of words to mean 'the same', **hetero-** is often added to the start of words to mean 'different'.

3. Complete the sentences.

Some alleles always have an effect. They are called _____ alleles.

Other alleles only show up if the individual is homozygous. They are called _____ alleles.

If an allele is recessive, you have to have two copies of the _____ allele to show the characteristic. [3 marks]

4. Mice can have different colour fur. The allele for black fur is dominant to the allele for brown fur.

a If a mouse has black fur, which of the following statements must be true?

Tick **one** box.

☐ The black mouse must have two of the same alleles, both for black fur.

☐ The black mouse must have two of the same alleles, both for brown fur.

☐ The black mouse could have two different alleles, one for black fur and one for brown fur. [1 mark]

b If a black male mouse is mated with a black female mouse, it is possible for some of the offspring to have brown fur.

How can this be explained? Tick **one** box.

> **Support**
> Don't guess. Read the information you are given. This will help you decide which answers are wrong.

☐ Both the black parent mice are homozygous for brown fur colour.

☐ Both the black parent mice are heterozygous for black and brown fur colour.

☐ The allele for brown fur is dominant. [1 mark]

Genetic variation

- The differences in characteristics between individuals are called variation.
- Some of the variation is due to differences in genes.
- Some of the variation is due to environmental factors.
- Some variation is due to both environmental and genetic causes.
- Mutations (changes in a gene or chromosome) cause new genetic variation.

1. Complete the sentence. Use **one** word from the box.

| genetic   environmental |

Natural hair colour is an example of _____ variation. [1 mark]

2. Variation can be due to genetics, our surroundings (environmental factors) or both.

Complete the table by putting a **tick** in the correct boxes to show whether the variation is due to genetic or environmental factors or to a combination of both.

Tick **one** box for each type of variation.

Type of variation	Variation caused by:		
	Genetic factors	Environmental factors	Combination of both types of factor
Eye colour			
Language			
Scars			
Weight			

[4 marks]

3. What is the name for a change in a gene? Tick **one** box.

☐ Chromosome   ☐ Genome   ☐ Mutation [1 mark]

4. When different gardeners grow sunflowers of the same variety, the plants have different heights.

a Is this an example of genetic or environmental variation?

_____ [1 mark]

b Suggest **two** factors that could cause the difference in plant height.

i _____ [1 mark]

ii _____ [1 mark]

Support
When the question asks you to **suggest**, you must think about what you already know and come up with your own ideas about the new information you are given.

Gene disorders

- Some disorders such as cystic fibrosis are controlled by only one gene.
- Cystic fibrosis is caused by a recessive allele. The person only has the illness if they inherit two copies of the allele that causes it.
- The alleles present for a particular gene make up the organism's genotype.
- The chance of inheriting a characteristic can be calculated from a genetic cross diagram showing how the mother's and father's alleles can be combined.
- We use a capital letter to show the dominant allele and the same letter without capitals to show the recessive allele.

			mother	
			Cc	
			C	c
father	Cc	C	CC normal	Cc carrier
		c	Cc carrier	cc cystic fibrosis

---

1. Complete the sentences. Use words from the box.

Genotype	Phenotype

a The appearance or physical characteristics of an organism is called

the _____ [1 mark]

b The pair of alleles present for a particular gene is called the _____ [1 mark]

2. Cystic fibrosis is an inherited disorder controlled by the CFTR gene. It is caused by a recessive allele.

In this question we will write C for the normal allele and c for the disease-causing allele.

a Complete the table below to show if each person is homozygous or heterozygous for the CFTR gene.

Person	Genotype of person	Homozygous or heterozygous?
John	CC	
Mark	Cc	
Angus	cc	

[3 marks]

b Which of the individuals above will be affected by cystic fibrosis?

_____ [1 mark]

c Complete the table below to give the possible genotypes (alleles) for each phenotype. Use the letters shown above. One has been done for you.

Phenotype	Possible genotype
Normal	CC or
Affected by cystic fibrosis	

[2 marks]

64

3. The diagram below shows a family tree. This is often a good way to show how an inherited disease is passed on.

Some of the people in this family have cystic fibrosis.

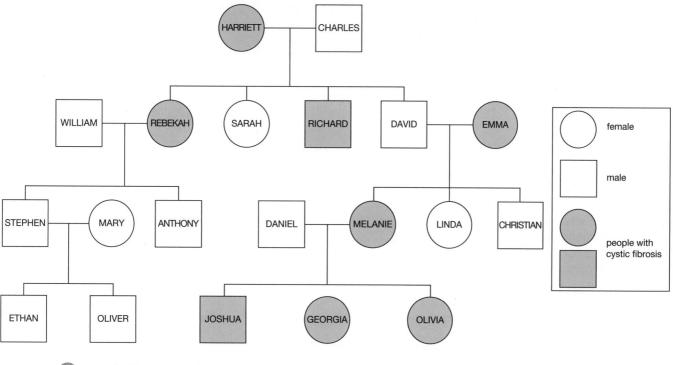

a Harriet has cystic fibrosis. Cystic fibrosis is caused by a recessive allele.

Give the genotype for Harriet. Use the letter C for the normal allele and c for the disease-causing allele.

_____ [1 mark]

b Give the names of **three** other people in the family who suffer from cystic fibrosis.

_____ [3 marks]

c Charles does not have cystic fibrosis. But two of his children do. This means that Charles must have passed on the faulty allele to these children.

Give the genotype for Charles.

_____ [1 mark]

d Write C or c in the spaces below to explain how Charles and Harriet's children could inherit cystic fibrosis.

The eggs made in Harriet's ovaries all have this allele _____.

The sperm made by Charles get either a _____ allele or a _____ allele.

When the sperm and egg cell join, a new cell is formed. The new cell could either contain these two alleles:

_____ and _____.

or these two alleles:

_____ and _____. [4 marks]

4. The diagram shows how the children of a couple could be affected by cystic fibrosis.

Complete the possible genotypes for the children of these parents.

Support
Vocabulary: A **carrier** of a recessive disorder has one copy of the faulty allele, but does not have the disorder themselves.

		Mother genotype cc gametes	
		c	c
Father genotype Cc gametes	C	_____ unaffected (but a carrier)	Cc unaffected (but a carrier)
	c	Cc unaffected (but a carrier)	_____ affected

[2 marks]

5. Polydactyly means having extra fingers and toes. Polydactyly can be inherited and is caused by a dominant allele.

The diagram shows how the children of a couple may inherit polydactyly if only one of the parents has the disorder.

a Complete the diagram to show the possible phenotypes of the children.

P = allele that causes polydactyly, p = normal allele

		Mother (affected by polydactyly) genotype Pp	
		P	p
Father (not affected) genotype pp	p	Pp Affected	pp _____
	p	Pp _____	pp Normal

[2 marks]

b Complete the steps below to calculate the probability that any of this couple's children will inherit the polydactyly condition.

Support
You can write the probability from a genetic cross like this one as a ratio, decimal or percentage.

_____

Of four possible children, number of affected

children = _____   [1 mark]

_____

Probability is _____ in 4 or _____   [1 mark]

Sex chromosomes

- In humans, one pair of chromosomes contains the genes that control whether a person is male or female.
- This pair is called the sex chromosomes.
- In females the sex chromosomes are the same (XX).
- In males the sex chromosomes are different (XY).

1. Normal body cells contain 23 pairs of chromosomes. Where in the cell can these chromosomes be found?

_____ [1 mark]

2. For chromosomes 1 to 22 the shapes of both chromosomes of the pair are the same. The shape of the sex chromosomes (pair 23) may differ. They are called the X or the Y chromosome depending on their shape.

Complete the table to show which sex chromosomes are found in men and women.

	Sex chromosomes (XX or XY)
Male	
Female	

[2 marks]

3. Use letters X and Y to complete the Punnett square to show possible combinations of the sex chromosomes.

Support
Another name for a genetic cross diagram is a Punnett square.

		Gametes in egg (from mother)	
		X	X
Gametes in sperm (from father)	X	XX	
	Y		

Show Me

[4 marks]

4. **a** Use the completed Punnett square to find the probability that a baby will be a boy or a girl. Give your answer as a percentage.

_____

= _____ %   [1 mark]

b Give your answer to part **a** as a ratio of boys to girls. Give your answer in the **simplest** form.

_____

Ratio = _____   [1 mark]

How features are passed on

- When a group of animals, plants or bacteria evolves, an entirely new species may form.
- Breeding that produces fertile offspring is not possible between two different species.
- All species alive today have evolved from simple life forms that first developed more than three billion years ago.

1. All living things have evolved from what? Tick **one** box.

☐ Fish   ☐ Simple life forms   ☐ Viruses   [1 mark]

2. Horses and donkeys are closely related but are different species. Which statement best explains why they are different species?

Tick **one** box.

☐ Horses and donkeys have some different physical features.

☐ Horses and donkeys cannot breed together to produce fertile offspring.

☐ Horses and donkeys come from different parts of the world.   [1 mark]

3. Donkeys and horses evolved from a common ancestor about four million years ago. Complete the sentences below to show how this might have happened.

Show Me

Individual animals in the ancestor species were genetically variable because of <u>mutations</u>.

In some habitats there were different types of living conditions. The animals best suited to each habitat

_____ and so were more likely to _____ and have offspring.

Over millions of years there were many gradual changes by the process of _____ selection.

Eventually horses and donkeys became different _____.   [5 marks]

Evolution

- There is always variation with a species because of genetic differences.
- Mutations add more variation by adding new alleles.
- Most mutations have no effect on physical characteristics.
- Some mutations have an effect that gives a better chance to survive and breed.
- Over time, there are more and more individuals with the useful allele.
- This is evolution by natural selection.

1. Name the process by which evolution happens.

_____ [1 mark]

2. Which statement about the effects of mutation is correct? Tick **one** box.

☐ Some mutations have useful effects.

☐ All mutations have useful effects.

☐ Mutations never have useful effects. [1 mark]

3. Giraffes are adapted to survive in their environment.

The theory of evolution by natural selection says that giraffes developed a long neck because animals with a longer neck had an advantage over those with a shorter neck.

Complete the following sentences. Use words from the box.

Breed	Clone	Food	Genes

A giraffe with a longer neck is better suited to its environment because it can get

_____ from tall trees.

Individual giraffes with characteristics most suited to their environment are more likely

to survive and _____ successfully.

The _____ that helped these individuals to survive are more likely to be passed
on to the next generation. [3 marks]

4. There are two forms of peppered moth, dark and pale. The dark form is caused by a mutation.

Usually the pale moths survive better because birds cannot see them on tree bark.

Air pollution in towns makes the bark of many trees black.

Explain why the number of black moths increased in polluted towns.

> **Support**
> This question is worth **3** marks.
> Try to write your answer with
> **three** steps. You could use
> bullet points, but remember
> always to write in full sentences.

Show Me <u>The black moths were less easily seen by birds, so</u> _____

_____

_____

_____ [3 marks]

Fossil evidence for evolution

- Fossils are the remains of organisms that lived long ago.
- Soft parts of the body do not usually form fossils.
- By studying fossils from different periods of time scientists can see that organisms have changed gradually over time (evolved).
- The fossil evidence has some time gaps. This is because many fossils have been destroyed, or are buried deep and have not yet been found.

1. Complete the sentence.

The preserved remains of organisms that lived long ago are called _____.   [1 mark]

2. Billions of years ago, the very earliest organisms had soft bodies.

Why are there are only a few fossils of these organisms? Tick **two** boxes.

☐ They have died out

☐ Fossils only usually form from the hard parts of an organism

☐ Many fossils have been destroyed by geological activity   [2 marks]

3. Draw **one** line between each fossil and the matching explanation of how it was formed.

| bones and shells | | The organism has not decayed because oxygen could not reach it. |

| dead animals or plants in amber | | The organs decayed and the hard parts of the organism have been gradually replaced by minerals. |

| footprints | | The animal left an impression in soft mud, which became covered in layers of sediment. | [3 marks]

4. Scientists have used fossils to work out how the modern horse evolved. The table shows some of their findings.

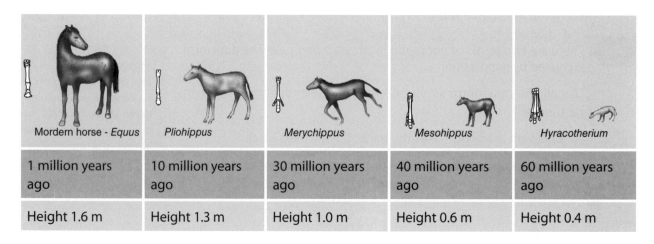

Mordern horse - *Equus*	*Pliohippus*	*Merychippus*	*Mesohippus*	*Hyracotherium*
1 million years ago	10 million years ago	30 million years ago	40 million years ago	60 million years ago
Height 1.6 m	Height 1.3 m	Height 1.0 m	Height 0.6 m	Height 0.4 m

a What conclusion can be made about the changes to these animals over 60 million years? Tick **one** box.

☐ The animals increased in height and increased the number of toes

☐ The animals increased in height and decreased the number of toes

☐ The animals decreased in height and increased the number of toes

☐ The animals decreased in height and decreased the number of toes   [1 mark]

b The animals are adapted to suit the conditions in which we think they lived.

We think the earliest horses lived in swamps or forests with soft floors, but modern horses developed as the forests dried out and became open grasslands.

Suggest how the modern horses might be better suited to living in open grassland than to swamps.

> **Support**
> **2** marks mean **two** ideas are needed. Remember, when the question asks you to **suggest**, you must think about what you already know and come up with your own ideas about the new information you are given.

_____

_____   [2 marks]

Antibiotic resistance in bacteria

- Bacteria evolve quickly because they reproduce at a fast rate.
- Mutations happen that make the bacteria resistant to antibiotics. The mutations become common because of natural selection.
- An antibiotic will not work against a resistant bacterium, so an infection cannot be treated.
- To stop the development of other strains of resistant bacteria:
  - antibiotics should only be used for bacterial infections (not for viruses)
  - patients should finish the course of antibiotics so no bacteria survive to mutate.

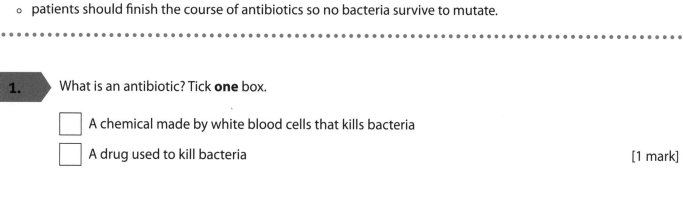

A population of bacteria. A mutation occurs.

A bacterium with the resistant gene(s) survives.

The whole population of the bacterium is now resistant to the antibiotic.

antibiotic treatment

1. What is an antibiotic? Tick **one** box.

☐ A chemical made by white blood cells that kills bacteria

☐ A drug used to kill bacteria   [1 mark]

2. Name the process that produces antibiotic-resistant strains of bacteria.

_____ [1 mark]

3. A lot of people stop taking their antibiotics when they feel better.

Complete the sentences to explain why it is important that if you are prescribed antibiotics you take the whole course.

Use words from the box.

Die	Mutate	Reproduce	Resistance

If you do not complete your course, not all the bacteria inside your body will _____.

The remaining bacteria will _____.

The more bacteria there are, the greater the chance that some will _____ and develop

_____ to the antibiotic. [4 marks]

4. MRSA is a strain of bacterium that is now resistant to most antibiotics.

Doctors are worried that MRSA could develop resistance to new antibiotics.

Sentences **A** to **E** explain how a population of bacteria develops resistance to a new antibiotic. The sentences are not in the correct order.

Put sentences **A** to **E** in the correct order. Two have been done for you.

A When a patient takes the antibiotic, the non-resistant bacteria die and the resistant bacteria multiply rapidly.

B Soon all the bacteria in the patient are resistant to the antibiotic.

C Eventually the antibiotic will no longer be effective.

D In the population of bacteria some have a mutation that prevents an antibiotic killing them.

E The bacteria spread to another person.

D → ☐ → B → ☐ → ☐   [3 marks]

Selective breeding

- For thousands of years, humans have used selective breeding to breed plants and animals for useful characteristics.
- They chose the best plants and animals to breed from, over and over again.
- This is how crop plants and animals kept for meat or milk were gradually improved.
- Examples include crops with disease resistance or higher yields.
- However, inbreeding can lead to problems.

1. Higher **yields** of a food plant mean more food can be grown in the same area, so the potential profits are higher.

Suggest **two** characteristics that farmers could choose to help breed an improved strawberry with a better yield.

Show Me

① Bigger _____

② _____ to disease

[2 marks]

2. Until the 18th century, most cows were bred for milk production. A British farmer then bred the first varieties of cattle that produced high quality beef.

How did the farmer choose the best parents for his breeding programme? Tick **one** box.

☐ The mothers had a high milk yield.

☐ The parents had thick hair to keep them warm in bad weather.

☐ The parents had more muscle than other cattle in the herd.

☐ The parents were gently and easy to handle.

[1 mark]

3. Describe how a new variety of cattle is produced by selective breeding.

_____

_____

_____

_____

Support
Remember, **4** marks means you must make **four** points. In longer answers you need to put your sentences together in a sensible order to get full marks.

You can use bullet points to help put your ideas in order but you must write in full sentences.

[4 marks]

4. Selective breeding is sometimes called inbreeding. Many pedigree animals suffer from health problems caused by inbreeding.

Suggest how dog breeders can prevent this.

_____

_____

[1 mark]

Genetic engineering

- Genetic engineering changes the genome of an organism by adding a gene 'cut out' from another organism.
- Genetically modified (GM) plants usually have higher yields or can resist disease or insect attack. This could help farmers produce more food.
- Some people are worried that eating GM food could be harmful to health, or that GM plants will reduce biodiversity.
- Bacterial cells have been genetically engineered to produce useful products like insulin.

1. Complete the sentences. Use words from the box.

Removed	Inserted

In genetic engineering, a gene is _____ from the chromosome of one organism.

The gene is then _____ into the genome of another organism.   [2 marks]

2. One type of bacteria has been genetically modified to produce human insulin. The insulin can be easily produced in large quantities.

Cow or pig insulin was used for many years to treat patients with Type 1 diabetes.

a State **one** disadvantage of using insulin from cows or pigs.

_____   [1 mark]

b Explain how using GM insulin overcame this problem.

_____

_____   [1 mark]

c Describe how bacteria can be modified to produce human insulin.

_____

_____   [2 marks]

Support
Remember, to get full marks you must put your sentences in a sensible order. Think about what happens first, then what happens next.

3. A variety of soya bean has been genetically modified to be resistant to herbicides (weed killer).

a What happens when a field of this crop is sprayed with herbicide? Tick **one** box.

☐ Not all the soya bean plants are killed

☐ Not all the weeds are killed

☐ Only the weeds are killed   [1 mark]

b Explain why this is an advantage to the farmer.

_____

_____ [2 marks]

4. GM crop plants have been developed that are resistant to attack from many insect pests.

What is the advantage to the farmer of growing these crops? Tick **one** box.

☐ The GM crops do not need to be sprayed with pesticide

☐ The GM crops do not need to be sprayed with herbicide

☐ The GM crops do not need to be sprayed with fertiliser [1 mark]

5. a Some people are against the use of GM crops because they may lead to a reduction in biodiversity.

Suggest how growing GM crops that are resistant to insect attack could reduce biodiversity.

Show Me Other (harmless) insects may be killed so _____

_____ [2 marks]

Another argument against GM crops is that the gene for herbicide resistance could be passed, in pollen, to a wild relative of the crop.

b Why would the development of herbicide-resistant weeds be a problem?

_____ [1 mark]

Classification of living organisms

- Carl Linnaeus developed a system for classifying living things based on how similar their bodies or appearance are.
- All organisms have a two-part scientific name: the first part is the genus name and the second part is the name of the species within that genus.
- Very small, microscopic organisms called archaeans were originally grouped in a kingdom with bacteria.
- The newest system of classification has three domains: Bacteria, Archaea and Eukaryota.
- Fossil evidence helps make evolutionary trees that show how all living and extinct organisms are related.

1. How did Linnaeus divide species into different groups? Tick **one** box.

☐ Linnaeus used similar physical features to group the species.

☐ Linnaeus used genetic relationships to group the species. [1 mark]

2. The table below shows the classification of the domestic cat.

Level of classification	Level name
Kingdom	Animalia
Phylum	Chordata
Class	Mammalia
Order	Carnivora
Family	Felidae
Genus	*Felis*
Species	*catus*

a Use the table to give the scientific name for the domestic cat.

_____ [1 mark]

b The wild cat and the domestic cat are very similar. Scientists believe they belong to the same genus. What is the genus name for the wild cat?

_____ [1 mark]

c Lions and other big cats belong to the same family as domestic and wild cats. Which **levels** of classification do all these animals share?

_____ [1 mark]

3. Kingdoms were the top level in the classification system set up by Linnaeus. Today scientists believe there is an even higher level called 'domain'.

Draw **one** line from each domain to the members of the organisms that belong to this domain.

Domain	Members of domain

Archaea	Fungi, plants, animals and protists
Bacteria	True bacteria
Eukaryota	Primitive bacteria living in extreme environments

[3 marks]

Extinction

- Fossils show that many species have become extinct since life on Earth began.
- Extinction means there are no remaining individuals of a species left alive.
- New predators, competitors and diseases can cause extinction.
- Human interference can also lead to extinction.

1. The dodo is an extinct bird. Explain the term 'extinct'.

_____ [1 mark]

2. Dodos only lived on the island of Mauritius. Three hundred years ago, Europeans set up colonies on the island. They brought new animals with them.

Complete the sentences to suggest why the dodo became extinct soon after this. Use words from the box.

| Predators | Competition | Prey | Disease |

Cats and dogs were _____ and they ate the dodo eggs and chicks.

Pigs ate the same food as the dodo, so another factor was _____. [2 marks]

3. The fossil record shows some time periods when many species became extinct in a short time. The table shows the five most important periods when this happened.

Time (millions of years ago)	Approximate percentage of species destroyed (%)
445	60
368	50
252	80
201	50
66	75

a When did the biggest extinction of species occur?

_____ [1 mark]

b Why do scientists believe these extinctions were **not** due to human influence?

_____ [1 mark]

4. Some scientists say that humans are causing a sixth major extinction event. In 2013, a total of 71 576 species of organism were surveyed; 21 286 were found to be threatened with extinction.

a Calculate the percentage of species that are threatened.

Give your answer to **two** significant figures.

_____

_____

_____

Percentage = _____   [2 marks]

b Compare your answer to the data in the table in question 3. Do you agree that humans are causing a major extinction event? Give a reason for your answer.

_____

_____   [1 mark]

Habitats and ecosystems

- Living things interact with their physical environment to form ecosystems.
- A population is the total number of one species in an ecosystem.
- All the populations of the different organisms together is called the community.
- The space where an organism lives in the ecosystem is its habitat.
- All the species within a community depend on each other. This is interdependence.

1. Draw **one** line to match each key word on the left to its definition on the right.

population	The total number of organisms of one species in an ecosystem
community	The space where an organism lives in the ecosystem
habitat	All the plants and animals living in an ecosystem

[3 marks]

2. A garden pond contains water plants and many different animals like snails, frogs and fish. The plants provide food and shelter for the animals. They also add oxygen to the water. All the animals provide carbon dioxide for the plants. The snail helps to recycle organic matter for the plant to reuse. The fish will eat the snails and young frogs.

a Tick **one** box to indicate the **parts of the ecosystem** described in the text above.

☐ The water, the plants and the animals

☐ The plants and the animals

☐ The animals

☐ The fish

[1 mark]

b Tick **one** box to indicate **the community** in the text above.

☐ The water, the plants and the animals

☐ The plants and the animals

☐ The animals

☐ The fish

[1 mark]

c Give an example of **a population** from the text above.

_____

[1 mark]

d Describe how the plants depend on the animals in the garden pond.

_____

_____

[2 marks]

3. Give **two** resources that plants may compete for.

1 _____

2 _____ [2 marks]

4. Give **two** things that animals may compete for.

1 _____

2 _____ [2 marks]

Food in an ecosystem

- Food chains show the feeding relationships in an ecosystem.
- All food chains begin with producers (plants or algae).
- Producers are eaten by primary consumers.
- Primary consumers are eaten by secondary consumers, which are eaten by tertiary consumers.

producer   primary consumer   secondary consumer   tertiary consumer

grass ⟶ grasshopper ⟶ shrew ⟶ owl

1. Plants are producers. Which process do producers use to make their own food?

_____ [1 mark]

2. Animals are consumers. How do consumers obtain their food?

_____ [1 mark]

3. This is a food chain for a woodland ecosystem.

Oak tree ⟶ Greenfly ⟶ Blue tit ⟶ Owl

a Which organism in the food chain is the producer?

_____ [1 mark]

b Which organism in the food chain is the primary consumer?

_____ [1 mark]

c Which organism in the food chain is the tertiary consumer?

_____ [1 mark]

4. The blue tit in the food chain above is a small bird. It is a predator.

a What is a predator?

_____ [1 mark]

b Name another predator shown in the food chain above.

_____ [1 mark]

5. The greenfly in the food chain above is a prey organism.

a Explain what is meant by 'prey'.

_____ [1 mark]

b Name one other prey organism from the food chain above.

_____ [1 mark]

6. After a cold winter, the number of blue tits can be very low. How will this affect the number of owls? Give a reason for your answer.

_____

_____ [2 marks]

Physical factors that affect living things

- Abiotic factors are non-living (physical) factors that affect the number of living things in a community or where they live.
- Abiotic factors include light intensity, temperature, moisture levels, soil pH and mineral content, wind intensity and direction.
- Oxygen levels are an important abiotic factor for animals living in water.
- Carbon dioxide levels in the air are important for plants.
- Biologists use transects and quadrats to study the numbers and distribution of organisms in an ecosystem.
- Sampling allows scientists to get a good idea of the number of organisms present in a larger area.

1. What are abiotic factors? Tick **one** box.

☐ The living conditions in a habitat   ☐ The non-living conditions in a habitat   [1 mark]

2. Complete the sentences.

The total number of a species in an area is called the _____.

The places where a certain species can be found in an area is called the _____.   [2 marks]

3. Some scientists investigated the effect of sewage on stream invertebrates. They collected five samples of water from three different sites. In each water sample they measured the oxygen level of the water and counted the number of mayfly larvae.

Their results are shown in the table.

Location	Oxygen level of the water	Number of mayfly larvae in sample					
		1	2	3	4	5	mean
1 mile before the outlet	high	10	6	7	11	11	$\frac{(10+6+7+11+11)}{5} = 9$
Just after the outlet	low	2	1	0	0	2	
1 mile after the outlet	high	7	6	6	6	5	

a Oxygen level is an abiotic factor in the stream.

Name **one** other abiotic factor that might affect the number of mayfly larvae in the stream.

_____ [1 mark]

b Calculate the **mean** number of mayfly larvae in each sample. One has been done for you.

_____

[2 marks]

> **Support**
> To calculate the mean value, add up all the numbers and divide by how many numbers there are.

c Describe the effect of the sewage outlet on the number of mayfly larvae in the stream.

_____

_____ [2 marks]

d The **median** is another way to compare sets of results. Calculate the median values for the experiment and complete the table below. One has been done for you.

> **Support**
> To calculate the median, put all the numbers in numerical order. If there is an odd number of values, the median is the middle value. If there is an even number of values, the median is the mean of the two middle values

Location	Data put in order	Median
1 mile before the outlet	6, 7, 10, 11, 11	10
Just after the outlet		
1 mile after the outlet		

[2 marks]

e The **mode** value can also be used to compare results. Write the mode value for the results in the table below. One has been done for you.

> **Support**
> The mode is the number that occurs most often. It may not be in the middle of your data. There may be more than one mode value.

Location	Mode
1 mile before the outlet	11
Just after the outlet	
1 mile after the outlet	

[2 marks]

4. **a** Complete the sentences to explain how you would use quadrats to estimate the population of daisies in a field.

Use words from the box.

Divide	Mean	Multiply	Randomly

Place the quadrat _____ on the ground. Count the number of daisies in the quadrat.

Repeat in different parts of the field and find the _____ number of daisies in a quadrat.

_____ this number by how many quadrats would cover the whole field.   [3 marks]

b Complete the sentence to explain why more than one quadrat sample is used in each area.

The more samples taken, the more _____ the estimate of the whole area will be.

c Quadrats can also be used to look at changes along a line in one habitat.

What is sampling along a line across a habitat called?

_____   [1 mark]

5. Some students used a quadrat survey to estimate how many daisy plants there were in the grass next to the science building. They placed 10 quadrats randomly on the grass, and counted the number of daisy plants in each quadrat.

The results are shown below.

Quadrat number	1	2	3	4	5	6	7	8	9	10
Number of daisy plants	3	6	2	5	4	4	2	0	3	5

a Calculate the mean number of daisy plants per quadrat.

You should show clearly how you work out your answer.

_____

_____

Mean number of daisy plants = _____ [2 marks]

Support
'Per' means 'divided by'. The number of daisy plants per quadrat is the total number of plants divided by the number of quadrats.

b The students used a square quadrat with an area of 0.25 m².

Calculate the mean number of daisy plants per m².

This is the number of plants that would fill a square metre.

Support
To calculate the number of plants per m², divide the number of plants by the area in metres squared.

$$\text{Number of daisy plants per m}^2 = \frac{\text{mean number of daisies per quadrat}}{\text{area of quadrat}}$$

$$= \frac{}{0.25 \, m^2}$$

$$= \underline{\hspace{2cm}} \text{ daisies/m}^2 \qquad \text{[2 marks]}$$

Support
Check your answer is sensible. The area of one quadrat is less than a square metre, so you should expect your answer here to be more than your answer to part **a** .

In a second site away from the school buildings the students found the mean number of daisy plants per m² was 20.

c What effect did the science building have on the mean number of daisy plants per m²?

_____ [1 mark]

d Suggest an abiotic factor that could have caused the difference between the two areas.

_____ [1 mark]

Factors affecting population size

- Biotic factors are living factors that affect the number of organisms in a community.
- Biotic factors are food availability, competition with other species, predation by other species and disease.
- Changes in one population affect another.
- The number of predators and their prey rise and fall in cycles.

1. Some rabbits live at the edge of a field. The rabbits eat the grain growing in the field. Foxes eat the rabbits.

Draw a food chain for these feeding relationships.

_____ [1 mark]

2. The number of rabbits in a population is affected by biotic factors.

Draw **one** line from each factor to the example of how that factor affects rabbits.

competition		Pheasants and rabbits both eat grain.
predation		Myxomatosis is an infection that can kill rabbits.
disease		Foxes hunt and kill rabbits.

[3 marks]

3. The graph below shows how the population sizes of foxes and rabbits change over a number of breeding seasons.

rabbits ----- foxes ———

a Tick **one** box that best describes the rabbit.

☐ The rabbit is a predator

☐ The rabbit is prey [1 mark]

b Describe how the population of rabbits changes over time.

_____

_____ [2 marks]

c Tick **one** box to show which of these factors might lead to a decrease in the number of rabbits.

☐ Smaller population of foxes   ☐ Larger population of foxes   [1 mark]

d Compare the trends in the graph for the fox and rabbit populations.

> **Show Me**

Both populations show _____

However, the peaks for the fox population

_____ [2 marks]

> **Support**
> This is a **compare** question. Remember to use comparative words such as 'higher', 'lower', 'sooner', 'later'.

Adapting for survival

- Living things are adapted to survive in the conditions in their normal habitat.
- An adaptation can be a physical feature such as the shape or colour of body parts.
- Other adaptations include behaving in a certain way.
- Extremophiles are organisms that can survive in extreme environments.

1. A behavioural adaptation is an action that helps an animal to survive in its habitat.

Which of the following is a **behavioural adaptation** that helps polar bears survive in a cold climate? Tick **one** box.

☐ They have thick fur that traps air and so keeps them warm.

☐ They have hair on the soles of their feet to give them a better grip on slippery ice.

☐ Pregnant females hibernate in dens during the winter to project the cubs from cold and wind.   [1 mark]

2. Poison dart frogs live in the Amazon rainforest. The frogs have brightly coloured skin. The frogs also make a poison which is secreted (released) onto their skin.

Explain two ways in which their adaptations help the frogs survive.

> **Support**
> Remember, for an **explain** question you have to link your answer to a reason.

> **Show Me**

Adaptation 1 The poison on their skin

(How this adaptation helps the frog survive)

which helps _____

Adaptation 2 _____

(How this adaptation helps the frog survive)

_____ [2 marks]

3. The fennec fox lives in the desert where it is very hot during the day but cold at night.

Explain how each of the following features help the fennec fox to survive in a desert.

Support
You will need to **use** information given to you and not just repeat it.

a The fennec fox is nocturnal and only goes out at night.

Show Me

It is cooler at night, so _____

_____ [1 mark]

b It has large ears.

Large ears have a large surface area so _____

_____ [1 mark]

c It has pale-coloured fur.

_____

_____

_____ [1 mark]

4. In some deep oceans, there are vents on the sea floor. These vents release very hot water and dissolved sulfur compounds into the surrounding water. Some bacteria are able to survive in the rocks and water near these vents.

Give **two** extreme conditions that these bacteria experience.

1 _____

2 _____ [2 marks]

Cycling materials

- Materials are recycled through an ecosystem so they can be used again.
- Water moves in the water cycle.
- Carbon is recycled through the carbon cycle.
- Microorganisms (bacteria and fungi) in the soil return carbon dioxide to the air and mineral ions to the soil when they feed on dead plants and animals.

· ·

1. Which process do plants use to make glucose using carbon dioxide from the atmosphere? Tick **one** box.

☐ Respiration ☐ Combustion

☐ Photosynthesis ☐ Decay [1 mark]

2. Name one process that releases carbon dioxide into the atmosphere.

_____ [1 mark]

3. Complete the sentences to describe the carbon cycle. Use words from the box. Each word may be used more than once.

| Feed | Microorganisms | Respire | Photosynthesise |

Plants remove carbon dioxide from the atmosphere when they _____.

Animals _____ on the plants and the carbon in the plants is absorbed into their bodies.

Both plants and animals release carbon dioxide back into the atmosphere when they

_____.

The dead bodies and waste from animals and dead plants are mostly broken down by

_____.

Microorganisms release carbon dioxide back into the atmosphere when they _____.

[5 marks]

4. If dead plants and animals do not decay, over many millions of years, fossil fuels such as coal are formed.

Describe how the carbon originally stored in the dead plants and animals is returned into the ecosystem.

_____

_____

Support
There are **2** marks here so make **two** points. Think about the names of processes in the carbon cycle, and if the carbon is as the element carbon or as a compound.

[2 marks]

5. Draw **one** line from each stage of the water cycle to its matching description.

| evaporation | | The water falls as rain, snow or sleet. Some runs off into the rivers and the sea, some enters the ground. |

| condensation | | Water is heated by the sun and becomes water vapour (a gas). |

| precipitation | | Water is taken up by plants from the ground. It is released from the leaves. |

| transpiration | | The water vapour cools, becomes liquid water again and forms clouds. |

[4 marks]

Pollution

- Biodiversity is the variety of living organisms.
- Pollution reduces biodiversity by killing plants and animals.
- Rapid population growth and higher standards of living mean humans are making more polluting waste, including
    - pesticides and toxic chemicals that pollute the land or water
    - sewage and the extra minerals in fertilisers that pollute water
    - gases such as sulfur dioxide that cause acid rain
    - methane and carbon dioxide that cause global warming.

1. List **three** pollutant gases produced by human activities.

1 _____ 2 _____ 3 _____   [3 marks]

2. Describe **one** human activity that causes acid rain.

_____   [1 mark]

3. Complete the sentences to describe how humans pollute the water and air around us. Use words from the box.

| Toxic chemicals   Gases   Fertiliser   Sewage |

Farms and water treatment works may release treated or sometimes untreated _____ into rivers and the sea.

If too much _____ is added to soil, it can get washed into rivers.

Factories and sometimes farms release _____ into rivers and the sea.

Fossil fuel power stations and vehicles release smoke and acidic _____.   [4 marks]

4. In 1911, there were 45 million people living in the UK. In 2011, 64 million people were living in the UK.

Use this information to suggest why the diversity of wildlife in the UK has decreased over the last 100 years.

_____

_____   [2 marks]

Support
Remember, when the question asks you to **suggest**, you must think about what you already know and come up with your own ideas about the new information you are given.

5. Traffic in our towns and cities is a major source of air pollution.

a Name an acidic gas produced by petrol and diesel vehicles.

_____   [1 mark]

b Suggest **one** way to reduce the amount of these gases released into the air.

_____ [1 mark]

6. Pripyat was a large city near a nuclear power station in Ukraine. In 1986 there was a nuclear accident and all the human population moved away. At first the animal populations fell as well.

Suggest **one** reason why the populations of many species are higher today than before the accident.

_____

_____ [1 mark]

Land use and deforestation

- Human activities are reducing the amount of land that can be used by plants and other animals.
- We do this by building, quarrying, turning forests into farmland and dumping waste.
- A lot of tropical forests have been cut down or burned to provide land to allow more food to be produced or to grow crops to make biofuels.
- We are also destroying peat bogs to make a cheap fuel and garden compost.
- Peat can store large amounts of carbon for thousands of years but this is released when peat is burned or peat bogs dry out.

1. Large areas of tropical rainforest are being destroyed to clear land for human activities.

State **two** uses for the land after the rainforest is removed.

1 _____

2 _____ [2 marks]

2. Two possible environmental effects of destroying large areas of forest are shown below. Draw one line from each effect to match it to the correct explanation.

Effect	**Explanation**
More carbon dioxide is released into the atmosphere	due to less photosynthesis, as there are fewer plants.
Less carbon dioxide is removed from the atmosphere	due to burning trees.

[2 marks]

3. Peat can be burned as a fuel. Name one other use of peat.

_____ [1 mark]

4. Peat is the only habitat for some plant and insect species. Describe how removing peat from the ground affects local biodiversity.

Show Me

Biodiversity decreases because destroying the peat destroys the habitat

used by _____ [2 marks]

6. Peat forms over thousands of years when buried plant material is not completely broken down by microorganisms.

Which of the following is a reason why using peat increases the carbon dioxide concentration of the atmosphere? Tick **two** boxes.

☐ The carbon stored in the dead plants is returned to the air when peat is burned.

☐ Methane bubbles trapped in the peat bog are released when peat is dug out.

☐ When peat bogs dry out microorganisms break down the peat, releasing carbon dioxide by respiration.

☐ The dead plants can no longer photosynthesise. [2 marks]

Global warming

- Levels of carbon dioxide and methane in the atmosphere are increasing.
- The increased levels of these gases contribute to global warming.
- Temperature changes will have an impact on ecosystems but there will be other impacts, for example due to changes in habitat loss and changes in food webs.

1. The graph below shows the level of carbon dioxide in the atmosphere between the years 1000 and 2012.

a Describe how the level of carbon dioxide in the atmosphere varied between 1000 and 1800.

_____

[1 mark]

b Describe how the level of carbon dioxide in the atmosphere varied after 1800.

_____

[1 mark]

2. Global average temperature has risen significantly over the last 100 years. In recent years, scientists suggested that the rise in carbon dioxide and the rise in global temperature were linked. A link between two variables is called:

Tick **one** box.

☐ an interaction   ☐ a correlation   ☐ a match

[1 mark]

3. Many scientists analysed data from all over the world to investigate the link between carbon dioxide levels in the atmosphere and global temperature.

   a Give one way the scientists shared their information.

_____ [1 mark]

   b Peer review is one way scientists check their work before it is published.

      Why is peer review by another expert important? Tick **one** box.

☐ To get an advance look at each other's work

☐ To make sure the conclusions are valid

☐ To check the information on the Internet   [1 mark]

4. Many thousands of peer-reviewed papers have now been published. The results show that carbon dioxide levels are increasing due to human activities.

Give **two** ways that human activities cause carbon dioxide levels to increase.

1 _____

2 _____ [2 marks]

5. Name another gas associated with global warming.

_____ [1 mark]

6. Before about 1800 the amount of carbon dioxide in the atmosphere remained fairly constant from year to year. Since about 1800 the level of carbon dioxide in the atmosphere has increased significantly.

Complete the sentences to explain these observations.

Until about 1800 the amount of carbon dioxide released by _____ was balanced

by the amount removed by plants for _____. There was little industrial activity

so the amount of carbon dioxide added from _____ of fossil fuels was very small.

During the Industrial Revolution and as the human population _____, the

amount of carbon dioxide produced by _____ of fossil fuels increased.   [5 marks]

7. Scientists believe that increased levels of carbon dioxide and methane in the atmosphere will lead to a global temperature rise. However, the amount by which temperatures will rise is not certain. This is because:

Tick **two** boxes.

☐ The atmosphere is a complicated system and we don't understand it fully.

☐ The atmosphere contains mostly nitrogen and very little carbon dioxide.

☐ None of the scientists agree.

☐ Scientists have to make assumptions about future greenhouse gas emissions.   [2 marks]

8. Give **two** reasons why conserving peat bogs and other areas of peat helps to reduce carbon dioxide emissions.

1 _____

2 _____ [2 marks]

9. Explain, as fully as you can, how sea level rise caused by global warming may affect both the distribution, and numbers of species living near the coast.

Distribution of species: _____

_____

Number of species: _____

_____ [4 marks]

Maintaining biodiversity

- A high level of biodiversity is necessary because each species in an ecosystem depends on the other species.
- Human activities are reducing biodiversity.
- We can reduce our effect on biodiversity, for example by:
  - protecting rare habitats that are the only home for some species
  - leaving hedgerows and uncut edges around fields where crops are grown
  - breeding species at risk of becoming extinct
  - reducing deforestation and carbon dioxide emissions.

1. Match the key words to their definitions. Draw **one** line from each key word to its corresponding definition.

biodiversity		All the plants and animals living in a habitat
interdependence		The variety of all the different species in a habitat
community		The different species in a habitat depend on each other for survival

[3 marks]

2. Maintaining biodiversity is important because each species has an important role to play in an ecosystem.

Suggest **two** ways that one species in an ecosystem may depend on another species.

1 _____

2 _____ [2 marks]

3. The Iberian lynx lives in Spain and Portugal. It became very rare during the 20th century.

Complete the sentences to describe how this species was saved from extinction. Use words from the box.

Captive breeding	Habitat	National parks

The Iberian lynx became rare because of _____ loss.

The Spanish government created two _____ to protect the habitat of the lynx.

A _____ programme was set up to produce young animals for release into the wild.

[3 marks]

4. Farmland wild birds are declining in the UK. One reason is habitat loss. Hedgerows have been removed to make large fields growing only one type of crop.

a Give **two** reasons why removing hedgerows would affect bird populations.

i _____

ii _____ [2 marks]

b Give **one** way a farmer could increase the number wild bird species on his farmland.

_____ [1 mark]

5. The table below shows the amount of household waste produced in the UK in 2012.

Type of waste	Yearly amount (millions of tonnes)
Metals	6.2
Glass and plastic	5.4
Paper and cardboard	3.7
Food and garden waste	6.6
Other waste	4.2
Total household waste	26.1

a Only 'other waste' cannot be recycled. What is the total amount of waste that could be recycled?

_____

= _____ millions of tonnes   [1 mark]

b Calculate the percentage of waste that could be recycled.

_____

= _____%

c In 2012, 42% of waste was recycled. How does this compare to the amount that could be recycled?

_____ [1 mark]

93

d Reducing waste by recycling helps protect wildlife habitats.

Why does recycling protect habitats? Tick **two** boxes.

☐ It reduces use of landfill

☐ It reduces biodiversity

☐ It reduces acid rain

☐ It reduces use of natural resources which helps prevent further loss of habitat [2 marks]

6. A biofuel, bioethanol, can be produced from sugar cane. To grow crops for biofuels, forests are often cut down.

Tick **one** advantage and **one** disadvantage of cutting down forests to grow crops for biofuels.

	Advantage	Disadvantage
Allows more food to be produced		
Habitat loss reduces biodiversity		
Provides alternative fuels to fossil fuels		

[2 marks]

7. Large areas in the Amazon rainforest are being cleared to grow crops for food or to grow crops to make biofuels. This benefits humans. However, there are also environmental problems caused by deforestation.

Explain how reducing deforestation in the Amazon rainforest will help prevent damage to the environment.

Support
Remember, you need to link your sentences together in a sensible order to get good marks.

You will also need to **use** any information given to you and not just repeat it.

_____

_____

_____

_____

_____

_____

_____

_____

_____

_____ [4 marks]

Section 1: Cell Biology

Looking at cells with a microscope

1. Cytoplasm [1 mark]
2. Nucleus – Controls the activities of the cell and contains DNA [1 mark]; Cell membrane – Controls the passage of substances into and out of the cell [1 mark]; Mitochondria – Where respiration takes place [1 mark]; Ribosomes – Where proteins are produced [1 mark]
3. Nucleus, mitochondria [2 marks]
4. Ribosomes [1 mark]
5. Resolving power [1 mark]

Sizes of cells and cell parts

1. $= \dfrac{20}{0.02}$

   $= \times 1000$ [2 mark]

2. Magnification $= \dfrac{7.5 \text{ mm}}{0.1 \text{ mm}}$ [1 mark]

   $= \times 75$ [1 mark]

3. a Real size $= \dfrac{\text{size of image}}{\text{magnification of image}}$ [1 mark]

   Real size $= \dfrac{3 \text{ mm}}{100}$ [2 marks]

   Real size $= 0.03$ mm [1 mark]

   b 0.03 mm $\times 1000 = 30$ μm [1 mark]

4. Real size $= \dfrac{\text{size of image}}{\text{magnification of image}}$

   $= \dfrac{4 \text{ mm}}{500}$ [2 marks]

   $= 0.008$ mm [1 mark]

5. $\dfrac{4 \mu m}{1000} = 0.004$ mm [1 mark]

6. $\dfrac{20 \text{ nm}}{1000} = 0.02$ μm [1 mark]

Cell division by mitosis

1. The two cells are genetically identical [1 mark]
2. DNA, genes, cell [3 marks]
3. Replicated, two, 46 [3 marks]
4. More cells are needed [1 mark] because the embryo is growing. [1 mark]

Cell specialisation and differentiation

1. A tissue [1 mark]
2. Long tail – helps the sperm to swim [1 mark]; Has many mitochondria – releases energy for movement [1 mark]; Nucleus has only 23 chromosomes – gives the correct number of chromosomes in the fertilised egg. [1 mark]

3. Differentiation [1 mark]
4. a The insulation means that the electrical impulses (or signal) are carried to the muscle tissues / are not lost. [1 mark]

   b The extensions allow the nerve cell to transmit the signal to many other nerve cells. [1 mark]

Stem cells

1. Bone marrow [1 mark]
2. Meristem tissue [1 mark]
3. Stem [1 mark]; specialised (or differentiated) [1 mark]
4. a The specialised cells [1 mark] produced could be transplanted into a patient to replace cells in damaged nerves. [1 mark]

   b Adult stem cells can only make stem cells from bone marrow / one type of cell / limited types of cell [1 mark]

5. a Produce cells of a certain type to replace damaged cells in the patient. [1 mark]

   b Cells produced by these stem cells are an exact genetic match with the patient's own cells. [1 mark] This means tissue grown from these cells would not be rejected. [1 mark]

6. Advantages: – stem cells can grow into many different kinds of body cells [1 mark]; in the future, stem cell transplants may treat diseases that cannot currently be treated. [1 mark]

   Disadvantages: any **two** from Embryos may have to be destroyed to produce stem cells; Injecting stem cells may transfer virus infections; Stem cells may grow out of control. [2 marks]

Section 2: Transport in cells

Diffusion in and out of cells

1. Diffusion [1 mark]
2. a The dye diffuses because it moves down the concentration gradient / from a high concentration to a low concentration. [2 marks]

   b Surface area of 1 cm block $= 6 \times (1.0$ cm $\times 1.0$ cm$) = 6$ cm^2 [1 mark]

   Surface area of 2 cm block $= 6 \times (2.0$ cm $\times 2.0$ cm$) = 24$ cm^2 [1 mark]

   c Volume of 1 cm block $= 1.0$ cm $\times 1.0$ cm $\times 1.0$ cm $= 1$ cm^3 [1 mark]

   Volume of 2 cm block $= 2.0$ cm $\times 2.0$ cm $\times 2.0$ cm $= 8$ cm^3 [1 mark]

   d Surface area : volume ratio of 1 cm block $= 6/1 = 6$ [1 mark]

   Surface area : volume ratio of 2 cm block $= 24/8 = 3$ [1 mark]

   e Decreases [1 mark], more [1 mark]

f i faster [1 mark],

   ii slower [1 mark]

3. increases [1 mark];

   large [1 mark]

Exchange surfaces in animals

1. a Oxygen [1 mark]

   b The concentration of oxygen is higher inside the air sac than in the blood [1 mark], so oxygen [1 mark] diffuses from the air sac [1 mark] to the blood. [1 mark].

2. Any **two** from: having a thin membrane, to provide a short diffusion path; having a large surface area; having an efficient blood supply/circulation to take the oxygen-rich blood away/maintain concentration gradient [2 marks]

3. To increase the rate/efficiency [1 mark] of diffusion/oxygen uptake. [1 mark]

4. a Increases the surface area [1 mark];

   b Oxygen [1 mark]; carbon dioxide [1 mark]; diffusion [1 mark]

Osmosis

1. a For both bags, the mass increases as time increases. [2 marks]

   b Water molecules move into the tubing from the surrounding solution [1 mark] because the concentration of sugar inside the tubing is higher [1 mark] than that outside the tubing. [1 mark].

   c 7.5 g – 5 g = 2.5 g [1 mark]

   percentage change $= \frac{2.5}{5} \times 100$ [1 mark] = 50% [1 mark]

   d 12.5 g – 5.1 g = 7.4 g [1 mark]

   percentage change $= \frac{7.4}{5.1} \times 100$ [1 mark] = 148% [1 mark]

Active transport

1. Active transport [1 mark]

2. Diffusion [1 mark], active transport [1 mark], active transport [1 mark]

3. Any **three** from:
Active transport needs energy to transport substances but osmosis does not; Osmosis (only) transports water but active transport moves minerals ions / sugars; Osmosis moves only one substance but active transport moves many different substances; Both methods move substances across membranes; Both methods move substances from more dilute to more concentrated solutions. [3 marks]

4. By active transport, using energy from respiration. [2 marks]

Section 3: Animal tissues, organs and organ systems

The digestive system

1. Liver [1 mark]

2. Tissue: muscle tissue [1 mark]; Organ: stomach [1 mark]; Organ system: digestive system [1 mark]

3. a Amylase [1 mark]

   b Any **two** from: stomach, pancreas, small intestine [2 marks]

4. Gall bladder [1 mark], stomach [1 mark], pancreas [1 mark], small intestine [1 mark]

Digestive enzymes

1. Enzyme [1 mark]

2. Products – The substances produced by the reaction [1 mark]; Active site – Where the molecule binds to the enzyme. Its shape must fit round the molecule closely [1 mark]

3. a Proteins [1 mark]

   b Carbohydrase [1 mark]

   c Fatty acids [1 mark] and glycerol [1 mark]

4. Carbohydrase [1 mark]

5. a Dependent variable = digestion time [1 mark] Control variables, e.g. concentration of amylase / mass of starch [1 mark]

   b Digestion rate at 20 °C $= \frac{5}{10} = 0.5$;

   rate at 30 °C $= \frac{5}{7} = 0.71$; rate at 40 °C $= \frac{5}{5} = 1$;

   rate at 50 °C $= \frac{5}{40} = 0.13$

   c The rate increases up to 40 °C [1 mark]; the rate then decreases after this. [1 mark]

   d The enzyme does not work as well. [1 mark] The active site has changed shape. [1 mark]

Factors affecting enzymes

The marks are in three bands according to the level of response. Level 3 (5–6 marks): Most of the information from the table is included and the method is written in a sequence that makes sense (not the order in the table) and could be used to collect valid data.

Level 2 (3–4 marks): Independent and dependent variables are described, some control variables given. The sequence may not be in an order that makes sense.

Level 1 (1–2 marks): The answer is weak. Some understanding is shown, such as what variables are controlled and what is measured.

The heart and blood vessels

1. Heart [1 mark], muscle [1 mark]

2. a vein [1 mark],

   b capillary [1 mark]

3. Aorta [1 mark], vena cava [1 mark]

4. a Arteries have an elastic wall so they can stretch when blood is pumped under high pressure. [2 marks]

   b Capillaries have walls that are one cell thick so they can exchange materials with the tissues. [2 marks]

   c To prevent blood flowing backwards. [1 mark]

Heart–lungs system

1. Lungs [1 mark], heart [1 mark]

2. (A), E, C, F, D, B [5 marks]

3. a Colour in the right-hand side of the diagram (containing blood from the lungs) red [1 mark]

   c Arrows on the left-hand side should be from the body into the right atrium, from the right atrium to the right ventricle, and from the right ventricle up through the blood vessel to the lungs [1 mark]

4. An increased surface area (or large surface area to volume ratio) [1 mark] allows more oxygen to be carried/absorbed [1 mark].

Heart problems

1. A device to hold a coronary artery open [1 mark]

2. Statins [1 mark], stent [1 mark]

3. By reducing levels of cholesterol in the blood. [1 mark]

4. Because the heart is made of muscle and muscle needs oxygen to work [1 mark]. Narrow arteries mean heart muscle does not get enough oxygen [1 mark]

5. a Benefit: easy for patient / does not require surgery [1 mark]

   Risk: drug may not work / may have side effects [1 mark]

   b Any **two** from: It is a long operation which could be quite dangerous; there are not many donor hearts; the new heart must be matched to the patient's tissue; risk of rejection [2 marks]

Risk factors for non-infectious diseases

1. It cannot be passed from person to person. [1 mark]

2. a Poor diet, smoking [2 marks]

   b Obesity, poor diet [2 marks]

3. a Correctly plotted points [1 mark]; Labelling the bars correctly [1 mark]

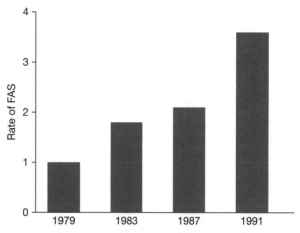

   b Rate of FAS increases with time (accept 'it goes up') [1 mark]

   c $3\,000\,000 \times \dfrac{1}{10\,000}$ [1 mark]

   $= 300$ [1 mark]

   d $4\,000\,000 \times \dfrac{3.6}{10\,000}$ [1 mark]

   $= 1440$ [1 mark]

Cancer

1. Carcinogens [1 mark]

2. Cancerous – Cells become this when they start to divide uncontrollably [1 mark]; Benign tumour – A slow-growing tumour, that does not spread to other body tissues [1 mark]; Malignant tumour – A fast-growing tumour that can spread to other body tissues [1 mark]

3. Increases validity: The scientists compared patients with lung cancer to similar people without lung cancer (controls) [1 mark]; The study was carried out with male and female patients [1 mark]; Other scientists have found similar results [1 mark]

   Decreases validity: The study looked at less than 500 patients [1 mark]

4. Environmental factors such as working in a dusty environment / genetic factors [1 mark]

Section 4: Plant, tissues, organs and organ systems

Looking at leaves

1. Leaf [1 mark]

2. Epidermis [1 mark]

3. Stoma/stomata [1 mark], guard cells [1 mark], chloroplasts [1 mark]

4. a Palisade cells [1 mark],

b Carbon dioxide [1 mark],

c Diffuse in through the stomata [1 mark],

d Oxygen [1 mark]

Water movement in plants

1. The root/root hairs [1 mark]

2. Increases transpiration rate: higher temperatures [1 mark], higher light intensity [1 mark] and higher wind speed [1 mark];

Decreases transpiration rate: higher humidity [1 mark]

3. f, a, b, e, d, c [5 marks]

4. a Any **two** from: thick waterproof cell wall; no cytoplasm; forms long tubes [2 marks]

b Very thin cell wall [1 mark]; large surface area [1 mark]

Minerals and sugar movement in plants

1. For photosynthesis. [1 mark]

2. Transpiration and translocation are both forms of transport in plants [1 mark]; However, translocation moves food materials but transpiration is the flow of water [1 mark] Translocation moves from the leaf but transpiration moves to the leaf [1 mark]; Translocation occurs in the phloem but transpiration occurs in the xylem. [1 mark]

3. Root hair [1 mark]; xylem [1 mark]

4. Active transport [1 mark]

5. a Phloem [1 mark]

b The cell walls at the ends of the phloem have many tiny holes [1 mark] which allow substances to flow from one cell to the next [1 mark].

Section 5: Infectious diseases

Microorganisms and disease

1. a Inside cells [1 mark];

b Toxins [1 mark];

c Cells [1 mark]

2. Measles and AIDS are caused by a virus [2 marks]; *Salmonella* food poisoning and gonorrhoea are caused by bacteria. [2 marks]

3. a After 40 mins: 1 x 2 x 2 = 4; after 1 hour: $1 \times 2 \times 2 \times 2 = 8$ [1 mark]

b 2 hours = 120 minutes; therefore, $1 \times 2 \times 2 \times 2 \times 2 \times 2 \times 2 = 64$ [1 mark]

Spread of disease

1. Measles [1 mark]

2. Link any sensible suggestion of method of transfer, (e.g. touching with dirty hands, vomiting, spitting) [1 mark]; with the idea of from someone that is infected to the food [1 mark]

3. Measles is spread by air [1 mark]; HIV is spread through contact [1 mark]; *Salmonella* is spread by food or water [1 mark]; gonorrhea is spread through contact [1 mark]

4. a Number of new HIV cases increases (accept 'goes up') [1 mark]; but the increase (in each of the 2-year periods) is bigger after 1999 [1 mark]

b No, it decreases [1 mark]

c 1700 − 590 = 1110; 1110/1700 ×100 [1 mark] = 65% [1 mark]

d 590 − 510 = 80; 80/590 ×100 [1 mark] = 14% [1 mark]

e Any sensible suggestion, e.g. people changing behaviour/ using barrier method of contraception/ clean needles for injection [1 mark]

Malaria

1. Protist [1 mark]

2. (C), D, B, E, A [4 marks]

3. a 1 100 000 − 440 000 = 660 000; 660 000/1 100 000 × 100 [1 mark] = 60% [1 mark]

b Fewer ponds mean mosquitos cannot breed as well [1 mark]. This means there are fewer mosquitos to bite people [1 mark]

c Nets prevent mosquitos from biting people sleeping underneath them [1 mark]. Insecticide also kills the mosquito [1 mark]

Plant diseases

1. TMV is a virus [1 mark]

2. The leaves on infected plants are patchy in colour pattern – because TMV kills small patches of cells and turns them white. [1 mark]

The infected plant cannot photosynthesise efficiently – because the leaves have many dead patches of cells. [1 mark]

The plant does not grow well. Crop yields are smaller – because photosynthesis is reduced. [1 mark]

3. a Spraying with fungicide – kills the fungus. [1 mark]

b Removing/burning infected leaves and branches – means the fungus cannot spread to other (unaffected) plants [1 mark]

4. Any **three** from: Same variety of plant; same size/ age of plant; same part of the garden / similar conditions (shade/sun); same soil / amount of fertiliser added. [3 marks]

Human defence systems

1. Hydrochloric acid [1 mark]
2. Seals the cut / stops microorganisms entering the body [1 mark]
3. Nose hairs / mucus in the trachea and bronchi [1 mark] trap particles [1 mark]
4. Any **two** from: can surround microorganisms and kill them; produce antibodies; produce anti-toxins [2 marks]

Vaccination

1. Antibodies [1 mark]
2. (D), E, C, B, A [4 marks]
3. **a** Both the number of cases and the number of deaths fell [1 mark]
   b 1970–1980: fell slowly / fell by about half [1 mark]; 1980–1990: fell more rapidly / much bigger drop [1 mark]
4. is reduced / goes down [1 mark]; stops or slows down [1 mark]; less / not [1 mark]

Bacteria and antibiotics

1. **a** Antibiotics do not work against viruses [1 mark]
   b Painkillers [1 mark]
2. **a** Vaccine (was introduced) [1 mark]; antibiotics (were developed) [1 mark]
   b 3700/5000 [1 mark] ×100 = 74% [1 mark]
3. **a** TB is becoming resistant to antibiotics / drug-resistant strains [1 mark])
   b Any **two** from: Only prescribe them for serious infections; make sure that the patient completes the course; do not use them as growth enhancers in agriculture.

Making and testing new drugs

1. Aspirin – willow trees; Digitalis – foxgloves; Penicillin – *Penicillium* mould [3 marks]
2. **a** Cure [1 mark];
   b Side effects/adverse reactions [1 mark]
3. To act as a control group to compare the effects of the drug [1 mark]
4. **C** [1 mark]; **B** [1 mark]; **D** [1 mark]; **A** [1 mark]

Section 6: Photosynthesis and respiration reactions

Photosynthesis for food

1. Oxygen [1 mark]
2. **a** The grass is eaten by the cow / energy transferred from the grass to the cow. [1 mark]
   b Because the plant makes/produces the food eaten by the cow (by photosynthesis) [1 mark]
   c Because the cow eats/consumes (the products of photosynthesis made by) the plant [1 mark]
3. **a** Respiration [1 mark];
   b Starch [1 mark];
   c cellulose [1 mark]
4. Glucose [1 mark] and nitrates [1 mark]

Photosynthesis equation

1. Glucose [1 mark]
2. Carbon dioxide – CO_2 [1 mark]; water – H_2O [1 mark]; glucose – $C_6H_{12}O_6$ [1 mark]; oxygen – O_2 [1 mark]
3. **a** Chlorophyll [1 mark];
   b Endothermic [1 mark]
4. chloroplasts [1 mark]; chlorophyll [1 mark]

Factors affecting photosynthesis

1. **a** Higher [1 mark];
   b Higher [1 mark]
2. **a** Count the number of bubbles given out **or** measure the volume of gas [1 mark]; in a certain amount of time / time given [1 mark].
   b Suitable range given, e.g. 0.1 m to 0.5 m [1 mark]
   c temperature [1 mark]
3. **a** Rate of photosynthesis at 0.2 m = 1.15 (accept 1.2) [1 mark]; at 0.3 m = 0.6 [1 mark]; at 0.4 m = 0.3 [1 mark]; at 0.5 m = 0.1 [1 mark]
   b Points plotted accurately [1 mark]; both axes labelled correctly with correct units [2 marks]; smooth curve of best fit [1 mark]
   c The rate of photosynthesis decreases as the distance from the lamp increases [1 mark]
   d A reasonable number from the graph – about 1.4 or 1.5 bubbles/min [1 mark]

Cell respiration

1. Mitochondria [1 mark]
2. **a** Oxygen [1 mark]; carbon dioxide [1 mark] + water [1 mark]
   b i Reactants: glucose, oxygen [1 mark];
   ii Products: carbon dioxide and water [1 mark]
3. Any **two** from: to keep warm; to move/work your muscles; send messages/impulses along nerves; allow chemical reactions to take place; growth/repair of cells [2 marks]
4. Oxygen – O_2 [1 mark]; carbon dioxide – CO_2 [1 mark]; glucose – $C_6H_{12}O_6$ [1 mark]; water – H_2O [1 mark]
5. Exothermic [1 mark]

Anaerobic respiration

1. Aerobic [1 mark]
2. Anaerobic [1 mark]
3. **a** Glucose [1 mark]; carbon dioxide [1 mark]
   b Carbon dioxide [1 mark];
   c ethanol [1 mark]
4. Three comparisons from the table; e.g. aerobic respiration requires oxygen whereas anaerobic respiration does not [1 mark]; both types of respiration use glucose [1 mark]; carbon dioxide is a product of both aerobic and anaerobic respiration [1 mark].
5. Carbon dioxide [1 mark]; 35 °C [1 mark]; enzymes [1 mark]

Effect of exercise

1. Glucose → lactic acid [1 mark]
2. Anaerobic respiration – Respiration without oxygen [1 mark]
   Glucose – The only reactant needed for anaerobic respiration [1 mark]
   Lactic acid – The only product of anaerobic respiration in muscle cells [1 mark]
3. **a** In the blood (red blood cells/haemoglobin) [1 mark]
   b To supply more oxygen / oxygenated blood to the muscles [1 mark]
   c To take up more oxygen into the blood [1 mark]
4. Because the build-up of lactic acid causes muscle fatigue [1 mark]; Anaerobic respiration wouldn't produce enough energy / anaerobic respiration produces less energy/is less efficient [1 mark]

Section 7: Automatic control systems in the body

Homeostasis

1. Amount/concentration of glucose [1 mark]; amount of water [1 mark]
2. Receptors – Cells that sense changes in internal body conditions [1 mark]; Coordinator – Receives and processes information about the change and brings about the response [1 mark]; Effectors – Muscles or glands that respond to the changes to restore normal levels [1 mark]
3. Glucose [1 mark]; body temperature [1 mark]; water [1 mark]
4. Muscles [1 mark]; glands (e.g. the pancreas) [1 mark]

The nervous system and reflexes

1. Receptor [1 mark], coordinator [1 mark], effector [1 mark]

2. **a** Bars plotted accurately [1 mark]; bars grouped with accurate labels [1 mark].
   b Students who are distracted/have noise have slightly slower/longer reaction times than students not distracted by noise [1 mark]
   There is no difference between the sexes [1 mark]
3. **a** In the hand [1 mark]
   b sensory neurone [1 mark]
   c Because the impulse/message [1 mark] bypasses the brain [1 mark] (no marks for just 'automatic' or 'takes a short cut')

Hormones

1. In the blood [1 mark]
2. Endocrine system – The group of glands that controls the body using hormones [1 mark]; Endocrine glands – Glands that make hormones and release them into the blood [1 mark]; Hormone – A chemical messenger transported in the blood [1 mark]
3. Labels are (clockwise from top right): pituitary gland, pancreas, ovaries, testes, adrenal glands, thyroid gland. One mark for each correct label. [6 marks]
   a testes [1 mark];
   b ovaries [1 mark]

Controlling blood glucose

1. Type 1 diabetes [1 mark]
2. **a** Pancreas [1 mark],
   b insulin [1 mark],
   c liver [1 mark]
3. **a** rises [1 mark]; blood [1 mark]; falls [1 mark]; pancreas [1 mark]; liver [1 mark]
   b The blood glucose concentrations rise for longer and reach higher levels in the person with diabetes. [2 marks]
4. Because body cells do not respond to insulin (produced by the pancreas) [1 mark]

Hormones and puberty

1. Puberty [1 mark]
2. **a** Female [1 mark], ovaries [1 mark];
   b male [1 mark], testes [1 mark]
3. **a** Any **two** from: pubic hair, underarm hair, voice deepens, wider/stronger shoulders, growth of testicles, growth of arm/leg muscles [2 marks]
   b Causes/stimulates sperm to develop [1 mark]
4. (C), D, A, E, B [4 marks]
5. Stage D [1 mark]

Hormones and the menstrual cycle

1. 4 weeks / 28 days [1 mark]
2. Menstrual cycle – The reproductive cycle in women, usually lasting about 28 days [1 mark]; Menstruation (or period) – The lining of the uterus comes off from about day 1 to day 5 of the menstrual cycle [1 mark]; Ovulation – The release of an egg from the ovary on about day 14 of the menstrual cycle [1 mark]
3. Egg [1 mark]; release [1 mark]; progesterone [1 mark]
4. Vertical line drawn up from day 14, labelled 'ovulation'. [1 mark]
5. a Oestrogen [1 mark],
   b Day 1 [1 mark],
   c Menstruation or period [1 mark]

Contraception

1. Fertility [1 mark]
2. Condom – This prevents the sperm reaching the egg. [1 mark]; Natural planning or the safe period – The man and woman avoid sexual intercourse around the time of ovulation [1 mark]; IUD – This is placed in the uterus (womb) to prevent the egg from implanting [1 mark]
3. a Ovulation date may vary / hard to tell when ovulation has occurred / sperm can survive for some time. [1 mark]
   b Spermicides kill sperm [1 mark]
   c It is permanent / it cannot be reversed / the couple can have no more children [1 mark]
4. You don't have to remember to take a pill / longer lasting [1 mark]
5. The marks for this question are in three bands according to the level of your response.

   Level 3 [5–6 marks] At least one advantage and one disadvantage given for both methods of contraception, and a reasoned decision is given. The evaluation is clear.

   Level 2 [3–4 marks] At least one advantage and one disadvantage given for both methods of contraception, but the evaluation may not be clear.

   Level 1 [1–2 marks] at least one advantage and one disadvantage given for one type of contraception.

Section 8: Inheritance, variation and evolution

Sexual reproduction and fertilisation

1. sperm [1 mark], pollen [1 mark], egg (cell) [1 mark]
2. a testes [1 mark],
   b ovary [1 mark]
3. a Fertilisation [1 mark]
   b The cell contains chromosomes from the father and the mother. [1 mark]
   c The single cell/fertilised egg/zygote divides by mitosis to produce many cells [1 mark]; The cells of the embryo differentiate / become specialised [1 mark]

Asexual reproduction

1. Asexual [1 mark]
2. Sexual [1 mark]
3. The new plant is genetically identical to the parent and the new plants on other runners from the same plant. [1 mark]
4. Sexual reproduction: two parents; yes, gametes are involved; yes, offspring are all different from the parents

   Asexual reproduction: one parent; no, gametes are not involved; no, the offspring are not all different from the parents [3 marks]
5. Genes [1 mark]; mitosis [1 mark]

Cell division by meiosis

1. Meiosis [1 mark]
2. 23 [1 mark]
3. 4 [1 mark]
4. Cell formed in ovary or testes – 23 chromosomes [1 mark]; Fertilisation – the egg and sperm fuse – 46 chromosomes [1 mark]; The fertilised cell divides by mitosis to form the embryo – 46 chromosomes [1 mark]
5. Mother [1 mark]; meiosis [1 mark]; chromosome [1 mark]; identical [1 mark]

Chromosomes and genes

1. Gene – A short section of DNA [1 mark]; Chromosome – A structure found in the nucleus of a cell that contains DNA [1 mark]; DNA – A molecule that has a structure of two strands arranged in a double helix [1 mark]
2. Genome [1 mark]
3. a There are genetic risk factors for some types of cancer [1 mark]
   b Any **one** from: Allows early identification of a problem; So treatment can start early; So preventative action can be taken. [1 mark]

Inherited characteristics

1. Gene [1 mark]; alleles [1 mark]
2. a The same/identical [1 mark]
   b Different [1 mark]
3. Dominant [1 mark]; recessive [1 mark]; recessive [1 mark]
4. a The black mouse could have two different alleles, one for black fur and one for brown fur [1 mark]

b Both the black parent mice are heterozygous for black and brown fur colour (and so it is possible for the offspring to have two copies of the recessive allele) [1 mark]

Genetic variation

1. Genetic [1 mark]
2. Eye colour – genetic factors [1 mark]; language – environmental factors [1 mark]; scars – environmental factors [1 mark]; weight – combination of both types of factor [1 mark]
3. Mutation [1 mark]
4. **a** Environmental [1 mark]
   b Any **two** reasonable suggestions, such as: environmental factors, such as different soil, different nutrients, use of fertiliser, different sunlight/shade [2 marks]

Gene disorders

1. **a** Phenotype [1 mark],
   b Genotype [1 mark]
2. **a** Jon – CC – homozygous [1 mark]; Mark – Cc – heterozygous [1 mark]; Angus – cc – homozygous [1 mark]
   b Angus [1 mark]
   c Normal – CC or Cc [1 mark]; Affected by cystic fibrosis – cc [1 mark]
3. **a** cc [1 mark]
   b Any **three** from: Rebekah, Richard, Emma, Melanie, Joshua, Georgia, Olivia [3 marks]
   c Cc [1 mark]
   d c [1 mark]; C or c [1 mark]; c and c [1 mark]; c and C [1 mark]
4. Cc for unaffected (but a carrier) [1 mark]; cc for affected [1 mark]
5 **a** pp – unaffected [1 mark]; Pp – 'affected' [1 mark] (in appropriate boxes)
   b 2 [1 mark]; 2 in 4 or 0.5 or 50% [1 mark]

Sex chromosomes

1. Nucleus [1 mark]
2. Male XY [1 mark]; Female XX [1 mark]
3. Top row: XX [1 mark], XX [1 mark]; Bottom row: XY [1 mark], XY [1 mark]
4. **a** 50% [1 mark]
   b 1:1 [1 mark] (do not accept 2:2)

How features are passed on

1 Simple life forms [1 mark]
2 Horses and donkeys cannot breed together to produce fertile offspring [1 mark]

3 Mutations [1 mark]; were more likely to survive [1 mark]; breed [1 mark]; natural [1 mark]; species [1 mark]

Evolution

1. Natural selection [1 mark]
2. Some mutations have useful effects [1 mark]
3. food [1 mark]; breed [1 mark]; genes [1 mark]
4. The black moths were less easily seen by birds [1 mark] so less likely to be eaten / could survive better [1 mark] so they bred more (successfully) / (more likely to) breed / pass on genes [1 mark]
   (accept for 2 marks best suited/adapted organisms are selected / are more likely to survive and breed successfully)

Fossil evidence for evolution

1. Fossils [1 mark]
2. Fossils only usually form from the hard parts of an organism [1 mark]; Many fossils have been destroyed by geological activity [1 mark]
3. Bones and shells – The organs decayed and the hard parts of the organism were gradually replaced by minerals [1 mark]; Dead animals or plants in amber – The organism has not decayed because oxygen could not reach it [1 mark]; Fossil footprints – The animal left an impression in soft mud, which became covered in layers of sediment [1 mark]
4. **a** The animals increased in height and decreased the number of toes [1 mark]
   b As the animals got taller, longer legs meant they would be able to move/run faster [1 mark]; they no longer needed toes spread out to stop the feet sinking in to the soft ground [1 mark]

Antibiotic resistance in bacteria

1. A drug used to kill bacteria [1 mark]
2. (Evolution by) natural selection [1 mark]
3. Die [1 mark]; reproduce [1 mark]; mutate [1 mark]; resistance [1 mark]
4. (D), A, (B), E, C [3 marks]

Selective breeding

1. Bigger fruit [1 mark]; Improved resistance to disease [1 mark]
2. The parents had more muscle than other cattle in the herd [1 mark]
3. Choose/select animals with the desired characteristics [1 mark]; breed from/mate the selected parents [1 mark]; select the most suitable offspring for the next cycle of breeding [1 mark]; repeat the process over many generations [1 mark]

4. Do not breed from problem dogs / make sure dogs are not closely related when choosing parents for a breeding programme. [1 mark]

Genetic engineering

1. Removed [1 mark]; inserted [1 mark]

2. a Limited in supply [1 mark] (also accept: ethical argument / obtained from dead cattle and pigs)

  b Unlimited supply as bacteria keep on reproducing / not taken from animals so vegetarians/some religious groups are less likely to have objections [1 mark]

  c The gene for making insulin is cut out from a length of human DNA/chromosome/genome [1 mark], then the human gene is inserted into the DNA/genome of a bacterium [1 mark]

3. a Only the weeds are killed [1 mark]

  b The farmer will have higher yields / greater crop production [1 mark] because of reduced competition for water and light between weeds and crops [1 mark] **or** save money [1 mark] because use less herbicide [1 mark]

4. The GM crops do not need to be sprayed with pesticide [1 mark]

5. a Other (harmless) insects may be killed [1 mark] so food chains are affected / insects/birds which eat the insects that eat crops have less food [1 mark]

  b Weeds become difficult to kill [1 mark]

Classification of living organisms

1. Linnaeus used similar physical features to group the species [1 mark]

2. a *Felis catus* [1 mark]

  b *Felis* [1 mark]

  c Family, order, class, phylum, kingdom **or** Felidae / Carnivora / Mammalia / Chordata /Animalia (all must be present for 1 mark) [1 mark]

3. Archaea – Primitive bacteria living in extreme environments [1 mark]; Bacteria – True bacteria [1 mark]; Eukaryota – Fungi, plants, animals and protists [1 mark]

Extinction

1. No individuals of the species are left alive [1 mark]

2. Predators [1 mark]; competition [1 mark]

3. a 252 million years ago [1 mark]

  b Humans had not evolved at this time [1 mark]

4. a $(21\,286 / 71\,576) \times 100$ [1 mark] = (29.7) = 30% [2 marks] (incorrect significant figures, max 1 mark)

  b Either no, because 30% is much smaller than the numbers in the table [1 mark]; **or** yes, because this is a very large number and may get bigger even though 30% is smaller than any numbers in the table [1 mark]

Section 9: Ecology

Habitats and ecosystems

1. Population – The total number of organisms of one species in an ecosystem [1 mark]; Community – All the plants and animals living in an ecosystem [1 mark]; Habitat – The space where an organism lives in the ecosystem [1 mark]

2. a The water, the plants and the animals [1 mark]

  b The plants and the animals [1 mark]

  c (The number of) snails / frogs / fish (will accept water plants) [1 mark]

  d The animals provide carbon dioxide [1 mark]; the snails help to provide organic matter [1 mark]

3 Any **two** from: light, space, water, mineral (ions) (will not accept simply soil) [2 marks]

4 Any **two** from: food, water, a mate, territory [2 marks]

Food in an ecosystem

1. Photosynthesis [1 mark]

2. By eating other organisms [1 mark]

3. a Oak tree [1 mark]

  b Greenfly [1 mark]

  c Owl [1 mark]

4. a Predators are consumers that eat other animals (not plants) [1 mark]

  b Owl [1 mark]

5. a Prey organisms are animals that are hunted. They could be primary or secondary consumers. [1 mark]

  b Blue tit [1 mark]

6. The number of owls will decrease [1 mark] because they have less food to eat [1 mark]

Physical factors that affect living things

1. The non-living conditions in a habitat [1 mark]

2. population (size) [1 mark]; distribution [1 mark]

3. a Temperature [1 mark]

  b 1 [1 mark]; 6 [1 mark]

  c The number of mayfly decreases after the outlet / by 8 [1 mark] but after 1 mile they start to recover [1 mark]

  d Just after the outlet, median = 1 [1 mark]; 1 mile after the outlet, median = 6 [1 mark]

  e Just after the outlet, mode = 0 and/or 2 [1 mark]; 1 mile after the outlet, mode = 6 [1 mark]

4. a Randomly [1 mark]; mean [1 mark]; multiply [1 mark]

   b Accurate [1 mark]

   c Transect [1 mark]

5. a (3+6+2+5+4+4+2+0+3+5)/10 [1 mark], = 3.4 [1 mark]

   b 3.4/0.25 [1 mark] = 13.6 [1 mark]

   c There were fewer daisy plants near to the building [1 mark]

   d Less light or water [1 mark]

Factors affecting population size

1. Grain → rabbits → foxes [1 mark]

2. Competition – pheasants and rabbits both eat grain [1 mark]; Predation – foxes hunt and kill rabbits [1 mark]; Disease – myxomatosis is an infection that can kill rabbits [1 mark]

3. **a** The rabbit is prey [1 mark]

   b The number of rabbits increases / reaches a peak [1 mark] then decreases / goes through a series of cycles [1 mark]

   c Larger population of foxes [1 mark]

   d Both populations show increases and decreases over time / series of cycles [1 mark]. However, the peaks for the fox population happen later / reach lower level than the peaks for the rabbits [1 mark]

Adapting for survival

1. Pregnant females hibernate in dens during the winter to protect the cubs from cold and wind [1 mark]

2. The poison on their skin, which helps prevent predators eating them [1 mark]; The colour (of their skin) warns predators not to eat them [1 mark]

3 **a** It is cooler at night, so foxes can hunt [1 mark]

   b Large ears have a large surface area so this helps the fox lose excess thermal energy / more blood can reach the surface of the ears [1 mark]

   c The pale-coloured fur reflects heat [1 mark] **or** the pale-coloured fur offers camouflage against predators [1 mark]

4 Any **two** from: high temperature; high mineral/sulfur concentration (will not accept salt); high pressure [2 marks]

Cycling materials

1. Photosynthesis [1 mark]

2. Either respiration **or** combustion (of wood or fossil fuels) [1 mark]

3. Photosynthesise [1 mark]; feed [1 mark]; respire [1 mark] microorganisms [1 mark] respire [1 mark]

4. As carbon dioxide [1 mark] through combustion [1 mark]

5. Evaporation – Water is heated by the sun and becomes water vapour (a gas). [1 mark]

Condensation – The water vapour cools, becomes liquid water again and forms clouds. [1 mark]

Precipitation – The water falls as rain, snow or sleet. Some runs off into the rivers and the sea, some enters the ground. [1 mark]

Transpiration – Water is taken up by plants from the ground. It is released from the leaves. [1 mark]

Pollution

1. Carbon dioxide [1 mark]; methane [1 mark]; sulfur dioxide [1 mark] (also accept other acidic gases, such as nitrogen oxides)

2. Burning fossil fuels [1 mark] (will not accept just 'combustion' or cars/traffic/factories)

3. Sewage [1 mark]; fertiliser [1 mark]; toxic chemicals [1 mark]; gases [1 mark]

4. Increase in the human population is increasing the amount of pollution [1 mark]; Increasing pollution kills more plants and animals / makes it harder for plants and animals to survive [1 mark] (will also accept: increase in the human population causes increased loss of habitat)

5. **a** Nitrogen oxides / any example of these / NOx [1 mark]

   b Any reasonable suggestion such as more efficient cars / restricted car use [1 mark]

6. Any reasonable suggestion such as less hunting / less pollution / less farming / more habitats available [1 mark]

Land use and deforestation

1. Any **two** from: land for cattle (for beef or milk) / growing crops as biofuels / rice fields / other food crops (allow only 1 mark for non-specified farming) [2 marks]

2. More carbon dioxide is released into the atmosphere – due to burning trees [1 mark]; Less carbon dioxide is removed from the atmosphere – due to less photosynthesis, as there are fewer plants [1 mark]

3. Compost for gardens / to improve soil conditions [1 mark]

4. Biodiversity decreases because destroying the peat destroys the habitat [1 mark] used by a variety of/lots of different wildlife (plants/animals/microorganisms) [1 mark]

5. The carbon stored in the dead plants is returned to the air when peat is burned. [1 mark]; When peat bogs dry out microorganisms break down the peat, releasing carbon dioxide by respiration. [1 mark]

Global warming

1. **a** Approximately constant / the same / fluctuates around a constant level [1 mark]

   b It rises (steeply) [1 mark]

2. a correlation [1 mark]

3. **a** Any **one** from: (scientific) papers / journals / publications / meetings / the Internet [1 mark]

   b To make sure the conclusions are valid [1 mark]

4. Any **two** from: combustion or burning of fossil fuels / deforestation / destruction of peat bogs or other areas of peat [2 marks]

5. Methane [1 mark]

6. Respiration [1 mark]; photosynthesis [1 mark]; combustion [1 mark]; increased [1 mark]; combustion [1 mark]

7. The atmosphere is a complicated system and we don't understand it fully [1 mark]; scientists have to make assumptions about future greenhouse gas emissions [1 mark]

8. Not burning peat keeps carbon stored in the peat [1 mark]; not draining peat prevents decay of peat by microorganisms [1 mark]

9. Any reasonable point with an explanation, such as

   Distribution of species: species move inland to new habitats [1 mark] because habitat is destroyed/damaged/flooded/too salty / conditions are no longer suitable / species cannot adapt [1 mark]

   Number of species: fewer species / reduced biodiversity / extinction of some species [1 mark] because less food available / habitat/nesting area/shelter destroyed [1 mark]

Maintaining biodiversity

1. Biodiversity – The variety of all the different species in a habitat [1 mark]; Interdependence – The different species in a habitat depend on each other for survival [1 mark]; Community – All the plants and animals living in a habitat [1 mark]

2. Any **two** from: food, shelter, pollinating flowers [2 marks]

3. Habitat [1 mark]; national parks [1 mark]; captive breeding [1 mark]

4. **a** Any **two** from: fewer sites for nesting / fewer sites for shelter / fewer insects or plants to feed on [2 marks]

   b Any **one** from: replant hedgerows / leave some fields uncultivated / leave margins at the edge of fields [1 mark]

5. **a** 21.9 millions of tonnes [1 mark]

   b (21.9/26.1 =) 83.9% [1 mark]

   c We are recycling much less than we could / we are recycling about 50% of what could be recycled [1 mark]

   d It reduces use of landfill [1 mark]; it reduces use of natural resources, which helps prevent further loss of habitat [1 mark]

6. Advantage – provides alternative fuels to fossil fuels [1 mark]; Disadvantage – habitat loss reduces biodiversity [1 mark]

7. Any **four** reasonable points, such as: prevents loss of (forest) habitat; prevents loss of biodiversity / extinction; prevents damage to food chains; reduces carbon dioxide emissions (less carbon dioxide released into the atmosphere from burning trees; more carbon dioxide removed from the atmosphere, as trees are left in the forest); so less temperature or rainfall change caused by global warming; less use of pesticides and herbicides from agriculture [4 marks]